ANTHONY CRONIN
COLLECTED POEMS

NEW
ISLAND

ANTHONY CRONIN COLLECTED POEMS
First published 2004
by New Island
2 Brookside
Dundrum Road
Dublin 14
www.newisland.ie

This edition printed 2005

ISBN 1 904301 55 X

British Library Cataloguing in Publication Data. A CIP catalogue record for this book is available from the
British Library.

Typeset by New Island
Cover design by Fidelma Slattery @ New Island
Printed in Ireland by ColourBooks

New Island received financial assistance from
The Arts Council (An Chomhairle Ealaíon), Dublin, Ireland.

10 9 8 7 6 5 4 3 2 1

for Anne
without whom ...

AUTHOR'S NOTE

The order of these poems is only very roughly chronological, as I feel that an arrangement which takes some account of the themes of poems has more attractions for the general reader. What seemed to me in retrospect to be avoidable faults of expression and versification have led me to do some re-working and revising here and there. I have removed a few lines from one poem, *Letter to an Englishman*, which I think now were expressions of mere opinion; but I have nowhere tried to make any of my former selves seem wiser than in fact they were. As I had intended at the time of its first publication in 1989, *The End of the Modern World* has been expanded and re-ordered a little. The previously uncollected poems included have appeared in *Poetry Ireland, Conversation Piece, The Sunday Independent, The Honest Ulsterman* and *The Shop*. Cordial acknowledgements are made to the editors.

Anthony Cronin
Dublin, 2004

CONTENTS

EPITAPH

Waverer, wanderer, weary at last
Of dallying days and of nights without rest.
No more now the winged one, so fearlessly soaring,
The lost one, uncertain, in loneliness faring.
The wishful, the wayward, in love with the longing,
With dream and with evening, the song and the singing.

FOR A FATHER

With the exact length and pace of his father's stride
The son walks,
Echoes and intonations of his father's speech
Are heard when he talks.

Once when the table was tall,
And the chair a wood,
He absorbed his father's smile and carefully copied
The way that he stood.

He grew into exile slowly,
With pride and remorse,
In some ways better than his begetters,
In others, worse,

And now, having chosen, with strangers,
Half glad of his choice,
He smiles with his father's hesitant smile
And speaks with his voice.

LIKING CORNERS

Liking corners, that is to say to know
Nothing unlimited safe, but even dread
Make warm when walled away, nocturnal storm
Bring walls and stove and books about the bed.

And to have often played in undertones,
Probably in small families and still
Have some peculiar games and monologues.
Be happy too with vacant hours to fill

Where corners collect the gold-dust of the sun:
Warm brick, warm fingered stone and bits of glass,
Minute particulars all afternoon,
Cool forest glades beneath the blades of grass.

At ten preferred to play indoors unless
The game could be a corner or a shed,
Liked musty smells and in a dormitory
Envied the one who had the corner bed.

The adolescent lying that no corner
Exists where dust and sun have made a hoard
Is traitor to this happiness, excitements
Of the orthodox and violently bored

Become him like his awkward gait, pretending
As the introvert can all too easily do,
The lout may long forget and hard remember
To what his popularity is due.

We take so long to grow and lie so often,
Absurd becomings, yet abysmal pain,
Corner boys lounging through a summer Sunday
Who must both find and be themselves again.

To find, yet hide, remain and still discover
Defines our truth. Through it alone we grow
Without a gruff betrayal of the secret
Safe in the corner that we yet forego.

WRITING

Our happiness is easily wronged by speech,
Being complete like silence, globed like summer,
Without extension in regret or wish.
Outside that sky are all our past and future.

So in those moments when we can imagine
The almost perfect, nearly true, we keep
The words away from it, content with knowledge,
Naming it only as we fall asleep.

In suffering we call out for another,
Describing with a desperate precision.
We must be sure that this is how all suffer.

Or be alone forever with the pain,
And all our search for words is one assertion:
You would forgive me if I could explain.

PROPHET

When word came back to that small whitewashed village,
Strange rumours of his ways and of his talk,
The neighbours shook their heads and didn't wonder,
His mother was bewildered more than proud.
And coming into lamplit towns at evening,
Seeing the warm red glow behind the blinds,
Lying awake in strange rooms above rivers,
He thought he would be like them if he could.

And when at last the courteous powers took notice
And nailed him to that awful point in time,
He knew that what he meant would be forgotten
Except by some as lonely as himself.

APOLOGY

It was proper for them, awaking in ordered houses,
Among russet walls where fruit grew ripe to the hand,
Walking on lawns where fountains arched in the summer,
To praise through their gentle days the dwelling virtues
And architect epics to honour the good and the brave.
And easy perhaps for the desert maddened preacher,
With his withered loins and the dirt hard in his pores,
To lash with his locust-tongue the uncertainly happy
And call on the townsmen to shrive and to shrivel for God.
But we who have climbed to the top of tall houses in winter
And heard in the gathering silence the limp of the clock,
Who dunned by our need through the days are unfailingly
   traitors.
In sad and undignified ways to each circle of friends,
How we can praise in our poems the simplified heroes,
Or urge to the truth we can never be true to ourselves?
O love that forgives because needing forgiveness also,
Forgive us that we have not lived through a virtuous day,
That we ask to be judged in the end by our own compassion,
Thief calling to thief from his cross with no Christ in between.

LINES FOR A PAINTER

The tree grew under your hand one day,
So many shades of green growing over the white
Canvas, as through the actual leaves outside the window
And through the open window onto the canvas fell the light.

And I sat on the bed trying unsuccessfully to write,
Envying you the union of the painter's mind and hand,
The contact of brush with canvas, the physical communion,
The external identity of the object and the painting you had
    planned;

For among the shards of memory nothing that day would
    grow
Of its own accord,
And I thought I could never see, as you saw the tree on the
    canvas,
One draughtsman's word.

Only inside the mind,
In the rubble of thought,
Were the pro-and-con, prose-growing, all too argumentative
Poems I sought.

Whereas there in Camden Town
In the petrol fumes and gold of a London summer was the
    tree you drew,
As you might find anywhere, inside or outside the studio,
Something which was itself, not you.

Well envying I have said,
But that evening as we walked
Through the cooling twilight down
To the pub and talked

I saw what in truth I had envied –
Not in fact
That you were released from any obligation,
Or that the act

Of painting was less or more objective
Than thinking the word –
But that, like poems, your painting
Was of course the reward

Of the true self yielding to appearances
Outside its power
While still in the dominion of love asseverating
Its absolute hour.

PRESUMING TO ADVISE

To have one's proper pride is right:
You were, and are: have grown, will come
To say what fools we were last spring
And will again discuss your youth undone
By talk and rainy mornings with a book.

Though there were days
When light ebbed without living, night
Was a bitter end to day,
Reminding how we once,
When coming home at evening, saw
Still in the field above the mill-race,
Grass which had yellowed there all of an autumn ago,

Still you remember,
Not like time or god to number conquests, as
Hay lies flat on the field in the summer evening sunlight,
Flowers droop in the glass when the lamp is lighted,
Not like that to number the used hours but say
Not this day's work, that woman's love, but
Here for all the years that were you stand today.

THE FUTILITY OF TRYING TO EXPLAIN

To explain is impossible, all
You can do is tell;
And carefully too because
The hostile, watchful eyes
Of the witness who saw the event
Are present again at the telling.

Say, I do not know how but here,
In explaining or even describing the stammer is there,
The awkward, angular gesture, the sentence unfinished,
But in telling the way of the water,
The curve of the road,
And not metaphor now but image.

And for the telling must trust
The ones who are not bound in blame
Or too proud to admit that it might,
But prepared to imagine and know
That the ultimate why is in when
And what colour the sky.

No not out of honour or justice,
Affection or anything like, are betrayers of chances:
Say that he shied
In his fear of invisible things from the end of the action,
And then, when the letter arrived,
Could not say why he lied.

ODD NUMBER

Asked which hand for surprises he always chose the left,
And tossing coins called always odds or tails;
Stuck away in an attic among other oddments
Was a book with big print which had warned him that success
   often fails.

Though patently unlucky he attributed his misfortunes
Not to the powers of luck but to the fates –
Another crowd who upheld predestination,
Puritans, not to be tempted by any bribes or baits.

And he thought of God vaguely as another Odd Number
Who could help him to get even by a process of addition.
A trusting dependence also on tomorrow
Secured that his sins were always of omission.

Only one consistent quality can be ascribed to him with
   certainty,
His friends found that in one way he honoured every
   demand:
He knew human beings were odd and rarely did the obvious,
And the midnight confession he would always understand.

HUMILIATION

Likewise the acrobat and the naked
On cross or on floor are exposed
To contemptuous smiles. The nervous snail
Constantly risks a rebuff and the caller remains
Hesitant after the door is closed.

Is it so, after seeing the sunset,
To remember and blush with blame?
The timid lover, uneasy debtor,
The guest who mumbles his date of departure,
Will sunsets exempt from shame?

Or say then what should be thinking of,
If higher to think of saying,
Is it the throb of the blood, or be drunk drinking sky?
Perhaps contemplation of some sort
Or is it praying?

Perhaps in this as any other,
Now as at any time,
After the foolish word as after the great injustice
The only answer is courage
For which there is no rhyme.

For the scorner scorns:
Never asking for pity
The hero would carry contempt like wounds,
Becoming, according to circumstance,
Silent or witty.

THE LOVER

All journeys end some place, and he was happy
Waiting for it to happen; there would be
Suddenly at a stop somebody laughing,
And looking from the window he would see.

The scenery wheel into place, composing
The proper setting and a mutual need
At evening would draw words and hands together
Until a love in doubt was love indeed.

But when he came where bands and tourists gathered
And she was there he found himself afraid,
And fumbled for that more successful other
And watched the one who loved her most recede,

As in stepped once again the sad impostor
Who had stood in for him many times before,
The capable, the talkative, the clever,
Who thought his real self was such a bore

He would not even trust him in the moment
When the great clock of night shook warnings down
Of mornings which would come for every lover
When all but the sad daylight would be gone.

And through the days that followed he deceived her
About the waiting self behind his pride,
The self that stood there humbly, like a landscape,
Finding its plea for love again denied.

ENCOUNTER

There were two suns – the second, on the water,
splintered and splashed by every oar and cry.
The mountains hung about like clouds and filled
the noon-hot sky.

Idly I flicked the pebbles towards the lake,
idly my words disguised the fear that lay
behind them, if you went, although apologising,
you would take with you the day.

Simply and solely for a moment there,
on those uneven steps, by that lake's side,
all that was other than I was you were,
all that was lacking in my luck for pride.

and when in autumnal London I await
more than a liking brings, the rain will drip
each day from skies like station roofs and still
that lakeshore wave will curl a mocking lip.

ELEGY FOR THE NIGHTBOUND

Tonight in the cold I know most of the living are waiting
For a miracle great as if suddenly ageing money
Repented its rule of the world, all, all of us failing
To find the word which unlocks and would give us something
Better than truth or justice.
And always we find ourselves wanting though all of us enter
The world as a humble supplicant and a lover
And the dream of the child is to grow at last to the stature
His love has attained.
I awoke one night in the mountains
And heard through the falling rain and the breathable
    darkness
The whispering world say, singular third person
We only know what you did we can never know what you
    wanted,
And not only wicked but foolish, Lord, are the fallen.
And now in the night when the city, gentle with neon,
Calls me from paper where love is an abstract perfection
To the village of friends who are gathered which none ever
    leaves
I must work out from the fractions of conversation
The total I answer for which is the total I am.

Yet tonight as the twig-breaking winter creeps in through the
    garden
And the blasphemous Irish are fighting on Hammersmith
    Broadway
The living pray to the living to recognise difference:
For who can believe that we are but the sum of our actions?
Only the saint and the dead and the deer and the dog.
We are what we want when we love though the wallpaper
    hates us
And tomorrows founder around a November in fog.
Though nothing remains as you turn to me now at the table
But a circumstance harder to cheat than the words and the
    white
Page upon which I will put down the poem I'm able
Instead of the one I will never be able to write,
I remember this evening how cold it was there in the
    evenings,

Two thousand feet up, the rain goose-flesh on the lake,
And the trees were black, the mountains gone and the rain
   still falling around me
Later when I the singular lay awake.

BAUDELAIRE IN BRUSSELS

Gas-lamps abandoned by the night burn on
Grotesquely as the daylight stirs the street,
And pain as bright as dawn behind the eyes
Is pulsing as the wings of madness beat.
The archetype prays to Poe to pray to God
For time to pay his debts and die of peace:
No mind can hold too many truths at once.
All contradictions cry out for release.
All contradictions: nothing equals pride
Except our hatred of ourselves: too late
God punishes in the person of his mother
One who endured before he chose his fate.

INHERITORS

For him the heavy-jawed and black-moustached
Who, strapped to a kitchen chair, will gaze
Forever from the school-book's page at guns,
And he who let us down in dying for
Another sod's poor dream; ask what for them,
What if at all can we,
Who know not any building's pride but pray
A clean bare place were grass returns and grows
When winds have taken ashes after fire?

CONSOLATION

Our Gaelic poets, going about the west,
Blinded with rage and sorrow
Among the sodden green hills, and feeling
The destruction in the wind,
Knowing that poor men's pride
Was only a drunkard's boast
And wanting a firelit hall
And a prince's head to be bowed
In acquiescence to the word;
They still must have rejoiced to find
Amid the fall of fortunes and the banishments,
That the careful also suffer with the gay,
In a time of trouble cute with the careless,
Having no guarantee
That next year, money,
However carefully hoarded,
Might not by a stranger's
Or by history's hand be squandered.

BALANCE SHEET

The dead men in their comfortable chairs,
Before the promotion crowned their smooth grey hairs,
Complained a little and complaining bled
Internally to death. Then got ahead.

But though the living still complain and say
That death is better, and though every day
They re-write sorrow in a furnished room,
The dead, if they showed pity, would presume.

How many hours of exultation go
To make despairing poems who can know
But those who lie till dawn beside their dreams,
Learning how different "is" can be from "seems"?

DUALITIES OF DESTINY

From up here all's landscape, lines of march,
Turning points in the rain, consequences taken,
Long dogged inchings, deliberate deceptions,
Lonely attritions perhaps, but ends not once forsaken.

Yet from down here are little but regrets and blunders,
Arguments as to aims, recrimination,
Sweating remorse, the goal so often talked of
Passed in the dark, no visible indication.

Down here are separate little deaths each day,
Running back to ask and calculating,
Fresh starts with less, dislike, unwilling settling,
Counting, recounting, forced forgetting, waiting.

Up here all's early omened, soon decided,
Seen in a word, a boast, a way of walking,
All ineluctable, following from the flaw,
The first mistake, its fair and fatal stalking.

SURPRISE

Since we are told it we believe it's true,
Or does as it's intended. Birds eat worms,
The water flows downhill and aunts depart.
Sea heaves, sky rains and can be blue.
Always love cherishes and firelight warms.
That knocking sound you hear is just your heart.

Nothing is angry long and all surprises
Are well provided for. The dog that died
Became a legend and then had its day.
Sooner or later someone realises
That a mistake occurred and no one lied.
If it is said to be then that's the way.

But soon when doors are opened hints are found
Of strange disorders that have no because.
In one room on the ceiling is a stain.
Someone is missing who should be around.
Some games are stopped by arbitrary laws
And an odd I does things it can't explain.

Nothing is order now and no forecast
Can be depended on. The thing declared
To be may not be so. The dear face wears
A false expression. Yet the very last
Surprise of all still finds us unprepared:
Although we say I love you no one cares.

EXAMINATION OF CONSCIENCE

There is no other answer but a lie
When once you know no walker can escape
The polished surface waiting for the eye.

Many are ruined by their honesty.
No cover then their shivering limbs will drape.
Emotional cheques will be returned r.d.

Misled by jingo orators we seek
To win from any abstract country pride,
But know that we'll be back at work next week.

Count up your sins before the others do:
That is a little though you always lied,
Swearing in drink that you would see it through.

I cannot say which murder cleared the air,
Nor which was courage and which cowardice.
They all assume the same defiant stare.

I know that one could always go away,
But do not think that would be good advice.
Life would begin again the following day.

FAIRWAYS' FARAWAY

At six-to-four and five-to-two
The sunlit winners raced
Across the green grass far away
While up and down we paced.

At Kempton Park and Redcar,
Impeccable and Strathspey
With summer all around them
Galloped through cheers that day.

Torn tickets, cigarette stubs,
Two up and one to come,
A square of sunlight laid upon
Dirty linoleum.

The third leg third at ten-to-one,
We blink in the light once more.
Cool consolation waits beyond
MacArdle's open door.

A dray rolls down South King Street,
The setts are warm outside,
A faint sea-breeze in Stephen's Green
Ruffles the typists' pride.

O endless August afternoons,
O grave reality:
Motes in the sun and melancholy
Stretch of eternity.

OUTSIDE

Outside, the day is all one could desire;
The valley full of bird-song, tractors, haze
And shimmer, heat for the first time this year
Broad on the back, and one could laze
Along and watch the water struggle free
Of last year's brambles, the old gate mouldering,
And, in the deep part of the lane, a bee
Bumble and nudge the rapt in flowering
Currant bush.

        That is if only you
Could get outside, if you could ever
Stand with the sun on your back as it is on the bark
Without hopping anxiously in and out of the view,
The day, the valley: completely sever
A second your link with your second-last remark.

OTHERS THAN US

Though choices they made once have left our friends
With coughs, false smiles and less regard, somehow
Our selves escape. For us each day suspends
Last judgement. We're still free to come and go.

Makers of settled history are they,
Mooching round four pubs with a famous shame,
Past ineluctable and at best a way
Of carrying on as if things were the same.

But we avoid finality. Small likes
Can turn out loss and leave us in for worse.
The lights just barely flicker when it strikes.
We know we'll soon have cause for fresh remorse.

Only in friends' disasters can we see
Finality and end: choice leave a mess
Forever, and we're still surprised when we
Find just how cheap life held their happiness.

SMALL HOURS

The clocks have different tones
And the night is heavy with rain,
As they lie awake in the dark
And go over it all again,
Re-shuffling reasons once more,
Equations of loss and gain.
Something when wrong they say,
Somewhere along the line,
Though this is the distant country
Where the sun should shine
To which in hope I travelled
I arrived here only to find
The same unpleasant companions
In the same frame of mind:
And life is lived in the present,
Encountering every day
Details that we couldn't
See from so far away.

And now in the rain-swept city
As the wind disturbs the night
They stare into the darkness
And wonder who was right,
Confusing fear with conscience
But knowing that they might
In some of those sad corridors
Which seemed to them the same
Where they stood lost and lonely
And took the proffered blame,
Have answered it with laughter
And so have staked their claim
To be with those who wouldn't
Not couldn't play the game
And a factory hooter blows.
In the wet grey morning air
As the whistling cyclists pass
Apparently able to bear
Daylight without remorse,
Recurrence without despair.

And they sleep in the widening dawn
Of a world which does not care.

REFLECTIONS ON FEAR AND COURAGE

1.
How can we feel our courage from our fear
When the baffling god who is not now or here

But sees our life's map in the future's round
(As even the dead may see from the rising ground)
Tries us by failure until, failure found,

Our nature which is formed by failure tries
No longer to compete in others' lies?

Granted the courage that the length of days
Imposes on the average. Grant also praise
And self-esteem. Remember that the ways

In which men prove or murder love are queer.
If no one else must face it, that is fear.

2.
Courage takes different forms.
Proust stayed in bed,
Emily Dickinson indoors,
Hawthorne stood on his head.

For his unpublished shame
Stevenson asked the Lord's
Pardon; and sometimes shame
Is only lack of words.

Unpublished courage
And unpublished shame,
Mere differences
Become the same.

3.
Anyway, take this for granted, that greyhead there you'll find
Talking of courage as constant, had neither hand nor mind.
A man comes to his courage through feelings by fear refined:
Confronted one day by a question and in affront striking blind
May forego fear and answer, but not leave it behind.

EXPERIENCE

Bored by the splendid view, assertive bulks
Of mountains blocking out the simple sky.
We turn and in a corner of the field we find
A shed reward the not-too-anxious eye.

A twig caught in a whirlpool on a stream,
The autumn sunlight on a rough brick wall,
These are the things I see although I know
They will not do for travellers' tales at all.

And once with some lead soldiers and some sticks
We built a city, ruled an empire, made
A few square yards of gravel give us back
More for our love than we've been since re-paid.

So all this drunken violence and noise
Is nothing. Though we're quite prepared to say
That it's a great occasion, still
I think we really wish we'd stayed away.

ANARCHIST

With dirty collar and shoes unpolished,
Dodging the traffic he crosses the street.
Thoughts of loose ends and unfinished poems
Drag at his indeterminate feet.

Now warm by the railings he saunters unhurried
Regarded by workers who fear to be late.
They have achieved like the ant to action,
His is a gloomier, lazier fate.

The bank will grow grimier, office blocks crumble,
The cinemas gleam in the April day,
But he has no part in the organisation,
For drainage or water-works he will not pay.

A bus shudders past him, he steps off the pavement,
Blood and world aging as onward he walks,
Now seated again at the marble-topped table
The dream flickers round him, he lives as he talks.

Tomorrow again perhaps wonder will wake him
And words like tame pigeons will flock to his call,
He will rise from the dead, this disconsolate lover,
And proudly and carelessly ride for a fall.

REALITIES

The possibilities that taunted childhood –
Step over distance and put back the clock,
I didn't mean it so it didn't happen –
Remembered afterwards return to mock

On Sunday evenings when we age most quickly
Such little livings as we ever earn,
And much bad weather falls before we really
Say with conviction what we're forced to learn:

That time is independent and that objects
Occupy space as they've a right to do,
That even on mirrored afternoons the wishes
Of any I depend as well on you:

And that a you is circumstance as real
As time or money or an act of State,
That circling in much circumstance we puzzle
Each other with a new and double fate.

All this I've learned and yet deny this evening,
And, for apology, can only plead
Contagion of your innocence restoring
The child's belief that all we need is need.

DISTANCES

Dear all the winter when the darkened seas,
The ship-borne lights, the miles of rain-swept tar,
The rushing towns, the mountains, the black trees
Were distance, I could think: it is so far.

Measure in miles the gap between our hands,
Say she sleeps now beyond the last shore light;
Then we lay parted like two friendly lands,
Alliance kept by engineers at night.

Those measurements abandoned now, apart
No longer so in space we speak at will.
But speech is measurement. We blindly chart
And speculate of seas between us still.

THE RISK

I hope that no lover yet
Approached the imagined good
But feared in his heart that he,
Dirty and scarred from the wood,
Might bring into that garden
Where everything holds its peace
And the gardening sunlight never
Foresees the end of its lease,
All the litter of crime,
Old letters, the rags and bones
Which every clearing waits for
As a glass-house waits for stones,
But from which perhaps in its silence
This green space might have been free
If he with a shout had not entered,
Tattered, anxious he.
And since my own disorders
The intimates I know,
Trail me as greedy companions
Refusing daily to go;
And insist the past we suffer
Can be contagious too,
It seems odd to say I love you
And to wish all this on you.
Except that like many another
Who glimpses the garden's grace
I cannot help also believing
That an intimate of that place
Who understood its enchantments,
But who knew there might be a day,
Illusory or real,
When crimes could come to stay,
Might persuade the fountain spirit
And the god of the bending tree
To close the gates to such bobtail
And set me suddenly free
And with such shadows turning
Away from the garden wall
Declare that a new beginning
Is possible after all.

MOSCOW IN WINTER

The Baltic shifts in avalanches and
The snow descends over the darkest city.
The plains roll on beneath a hunter's moon.
The flakes float from the gloom around the huge
And empty squares; the star glows red below
The murk of sky; silence inhabits the streets.
Crooked the black smudge inches through the slush
Under the Kremlin wall towards the tomb
Where marbled mummies clasp among the flowers.
Everywhere crowd the people who have been
An abstract of our lies and our despair.
These stubbled, patient faces still bespeak
The silence of the muzhik centuries.
Anonymously loved and tortured too,
Hollow the old men stare through history where
The backs bend low beneath the Rostov sky.
My shoes were leaking by the Kremlin wall.
The Don flamed red beneath our wing at dawn.
Dim lit, with rocking shadows, stretched the wide
Avenues to where human warmth crowded
About a stove, the hot and blowsy flesh.
The cold that evening turned the blood to whispers.
Buffeting snow the skyscrapers bulked through the gloom.
Muffled the cry of millions from the plains.
Muffled Bukharin's cry, old comrades why.

R.M.S. TITANIC
(1961)

I

Trembling with engines, gulping oil, the river
Under the factories glowering in the dark
Is home of the gulls and homeless; cold
Lights on the sucking tideway, scurf and sewage,
Gobbets of smoke and staleness and the smell,
The seaweed sour and morning smell of sea.

Here in the doss the river fog is dawn.
Under the yellow lights it twists like tapeworm,
Wreathes round the bulbs and, with the scent of urine,
Creeps down the bare board corridors, becomes
The sour, sweet breath of old men, sleepless, coughing.

Lights on the glistening metal, numinous fog
Feathering to mist, thin garlands hung
On the wet back of the Mersey. Out to sea
A great dawn heaves and tugs the tide past Crosby.

II

On the bog road the blackthorn flowers, the turf-stacks,
Chocolate brown, are built like bricks but softer,
And softer too the west of Ireland sky.
Turf smoke is chalked upon the darker blue
And leaves a sweet, rich, poor man's smell in cloth.
Great ragged rhododendrons sprawl through gaps
And pink and white the chestnut blossom tops
The tumbled granite wall round the demesne.
The high, brass-bound De Dion coughing past,
O'Conor Don and the solicitor,
Disturbs the dust but not the sleeping dogs.

Disturb the memories in an old man's head.
We only live one life, with one beginning.
The coming degradations of the heart
We who awake with all our landfalls staring
Back at us in the dawn, must hold our breath for.
The west is not awake to where *Titanic*
Smokes in the morning, huge against the stars.

III

No one spoke of this in the parlour bookcase.
R. M. Ballantyne held no hint of chaos.
There was no astonishing ship in the morning sky,
Slanting and falling in appalling ruin.
There was only the deliberate enunciation of an April Sunday
Announcing twelve o'clock:
A bobbined green cloth on the parlour table,
The prolonged anticipatory pleasure of a boy's boredom,
Church bells and baking smells, the buff and throaty hens.
A Protestant hymn vibrates in the musty sunlight,
Nearer my God to Thee, nearer to Thee.

O nothing so huge and wonderful as disaster
(Fenimore Cooper could have foretold that,
Or all of the foolish liars in the bookcase
Prognosticated something of the kind
In terms of a boy's heroics –
The long gashed hull, the officers, the boats)
But led by a cyclopedia to the slaughter,
Expecting a world of fountain pens and clippings;
And led like a romantic to the slaughter,
Imagining voices in the song-washed dusk.
O who in that bookcase foretold the derisive laughter?

IV

Those who lately took the notion
To cross the rolling and roaring Atlantic Ocean
Where the dead of the coffin ships once washed
To and fro on the shingle, shoals of corpses,
Ocean dividing the parishes of Bertraghboy and Boston,
Are battened now beside the pounding engines,
Oil and varnish floating on the darkness,
While it wanders like a headland through the North Atlantic,
Or like a city oscillating across a landscape,
Into whose basements the emigrants are crowded with their
    worries.
It is impossible not to feel for the poor of this nation
Sentiments of companionship and love,
For although the forgiving of misfortune is among the most
    dangerous of human operations,
In the alleyways of our need we turn for help
Not to those who judge but to those who do not care,
Companions now under the naked bulbs
In the communal forgetting of drunken consociation
Where the lies are allowed for an hour between one day and
    another.

V

Now Lightoller sees with pride the order of reasonable
  magnitude
Bulking and glistening round him, metallic, echoing,
As he stands on his bridge over vibrating darkness,
A capable man and therefore entitled to pride,
And truly also neither a bore nor a prig;
Or at least on this April night of nineteen twelve,
Standing decent and quiet under the towering smokestacks,
While the great ship, lighted like late-night London,
Moves towards a rising and falling horizon over the respiring
  ocean
Into disaster he cannot foresee, has no reason to enquire
Into the truth he might not be able to endure.
Mr Lightoller, last of the line, now, let us take you, of likeable
  men,
As you move through the cloud of the night with a cap set
  square on your head
And your responsibilities shouldered,
For it is possible that there were such simplicities,
A schoolboy autumn order with no rot at the core,
Without the knowledge of interior and exterior degradations,
The cracked voice, the face crumbling into that of a fool or a
  bully
And already that of a bore:
But there will soon in the habited world be only the blind and
  the ruined,
The active who, claiming to be just, are devoid of compassion
  and self-knowledge,
And those who will never act again, who tremble with
  disgust,
The half-men and the crippled, neither good,
Who demand from omnipotent god excluding dispensations,
Mercy and justice,
Or at best meet together in an obscene embrace
Like the criminal and the boyish police.
The limited man may act and judge, Mr Lightoller,
But prepare to incur some contempt.

VI

Down underneath the Irish poor are singing
Their songs of Philadelphia in the morning,
In comradeship romantically clinging
To those whom they would murder without warning.
A warm frieze crowd where every eye is crying
And all the songs are always of misfortune,
Inured to the snug, cosy slop of dying
They watch the grey rats creeping to the ocean.
Down here no one will judge, and all's forgiven.
Every man loves the thing he kills and slowly,
With many a tear the smiler does the knifing.
Down here the failure to redeem is holy.
Their songs of loss, of exile, desolation,
Hang on the wide still night. They shout of loving.
Each heart is full of black midnight emotion
And will create a sorrow for its proving.

Surely among the rich men's snowy linen
The dignified and decent can be found,
The stainless, crystal, cut-glass attitudes
And mouths shut on the boy's need to impress,
Instead of the hysterical moist palm,
The smiling urgencies of need and love,
The trader's charm, the clever one's reply.
Familiarities of skin and cloth
Clinging in fecundation to the sweat,
What won't wash out, the bit of shit on shirt,
The fungoid socks, the broken shoe, skinned heel,
The hanging round for hours, the aptly named,
Indeed intrusive, hand on shoulder touch –
Surely the rich, who know the tiny shiver
Caressing the dry, lonely, selfish skin
Contrive to keep some attitudes intact,
Reptiles who change, three times a day, their cloth?

Sick in the bilboes of the world the poor
Cling to each other, but the rich cling more
Closely to the cruelty that prevents
The dissolution of the modelled stance,
The waxwork melting of the features down,

The blubber sympathy when sorrows drown.
Oh if this face concealed great pain we might
Call it necessity and concede its right,
But, multiplied in the racing mirrors here,
The eyes of money, vacantly severe,
The polished surfaces, the silver knives,
The gorgon heads which model the good lives
Presume a reckoning from the weak, the odd,
The young, to proffer to a glutton god.
The face of justice does not mask its grief
But emptiness and greed and disbelief,
A solemn bully's face, pretentious, grave,
Loathing the brother that it fears to save
Lest money and attendance might not get
Their due reward, their prior claims be met.
To all the decent scriveners it lied
Who bit upon that coin before they died
And found it hollow and who took the blame,
Bearing their own, their son's and father's shame.

VII

A tragedy is only one mistake,
Or the last in a series, making all irretrievable.
The tragic accident is the one which leaves
The knowledge that a desired possibility has been finally
    destroyed
By neglect, foolishness, or bad luck.
When the shock ran back along the narrow alleys
The lights were suddenly darkened,
Bringing the consciousness of error.
But although the voices rose again after the silence
The lights did not fully recover.
Then the engines stopped,
For now they were in the interval between two events,
The irretrievable mistake in the past
And the inevitable consequence in the future.
And as knowledge of the nature of the mistake grew in each
    mind
So did the penalty loom clearer out of the small hours.

VIII

Who can make plausible what happens?
Only the inexplicable rules
Over the worst of our lives,
The intimate degradations,
The disproportionate punishments
For the trivial mistakes.
Loud in the echoless night
Titanic is not alone,
Also enclosed by the sky
The *Californian's* lights
Deny necessity
And dignity to its fate.
Around its boarded decks
Fear infects the dark,
Slowly its floors slop down
Into the freezing peace
Of the calm and ridiculous sea.
Lightoller clings to the real,
The world that cannot be regained,
And those lustrous lights shine on
Like the ordinary overheard
After the end of the world.
They call out for help, they wait
For the casual world to reply,
But the *Californian's* lights,
Cosy in great, cold dark,
Simply inform the damned
The households are happy and safe.
Over and over again
Their rockets flare through the cold
But no answer at all returns
As from an inanimate phone
Incredibly ringing on
While the seconds expand in the head.
They stare at a shocking thing,
Mankind untouched by their fear,
The *Californian's* lights
Like a pierhead glistening there.
Nothing can ever explain
This further grotesque mischance,

Redeem with cause and effect
Their aloneness inside the vast
Cloud which obscures the real,
Which makes their voice unheard,
Their foghorn shaking the stars,
Their rockets shocking the dark,
Their courage, their casual jokes,
Their anxious, ordinary talk.

Many at home will awake
To find this gigantic ship
Has sailed into the bay
Whose waves lulled them to sleep,
Preternaturally great,
Obscuring most of the sky,
While the darkness spreads overhead
As the great ship comes close,
The appalling shape in the bay
Towering over the house.

IX

Coagulate with cold and dark the sea
Sucks down *Titanic* as the hiss of steam
Dies over empty distance. The boats gaze
On what was home, eleven storeys high,
Commotion crowding on its decks, its lights
Tilting above them as the band plays on.

Is Horatio Bottomley who climbs now by the stairs
To the sliding platforms of the ship
Strength or weakness? Are the deceptions the late king
practised,
Flitting between the cabins, dishonour?

The freezing sea heaves slowly as it sinks
Into a tidal wave as high as it
Which licks the stars. The screaming rich sucked under
And the poor cry in that icy darkness
One last time, and then the cowering boats
Are hoisted up among the stars themselves.
The great ship gone the lucky count their loss
And search and search again to find the gain,
What guttered in the darkness of that wave,
For why else may the living not believe
The lies that served the first-class passengers
As passports to redemption from the dirt?

Under soft showers of April lies the west,
Belled washed-out skies, the angelus, drenched birds.
Before our fathers stretches nineteen twelve,
The cloudy evenings and the river pools.
The freemen's journals soon will tell the story
And life rub in the lesson day by day.
There is no decency except a lie.

47

X

The hot breath of the brass, the drum's insistence,
Tar-barrels flaming in the market square,
And then the declinations of the heart.
Troubled by drums and scent the blood is trembling,
And caverned under canvas, taunting, white,
The girls twist, sensuously touched by light.

Rain beats on the branches, scattering
Debris of April, blossoms and leaves on the ground.
Petals and twigs afloat on the sky in the roadway,
Deciduous stonework black as the big house crumbles,
The roofs with afterglow of rain still bright,
Auguring autumns to come in a cold light.

We live by living, survive by mere surviving.
Stubborn beyond our stubbornness or strength
Our virtues, like our weaknesses, prevail.
A man may suffer goodness like a growth
Intimate with his life. See, in his face
His gentleness encounter its disgrace.

Industrialisation ?

The dreams born in the mists of autumn evenings,
Cold, blue, tingling leaf-falls after rugby,
With lights in passing buses: promises:
Remembrances of wrongs in mothers' eyes:
Money's smooth hum: migrating newspapers
Flocking across the skies: the cameras purring
On whores' ecstasies of self-possession:
Insane and fearful punctualities
Will keep the bands still playing, the great ship
Towering above the roadsteads of the world.
And they will bless the Pope this time in building
It in a Belfast of exorbitant virtue,
Bound still by decent business's iron tramlines.

As the world drifts with dismal Sunday bells
Into an April half a century on,
Sweating awake, their skin next to the blankets,
Many reflect on how their lives were not
As once imagined. Sepia photographs
Whose background was a swathe of shimmering sea,
Gone, with the cupboards, washstands, bedroom ceilings
Under which decencies perished hour by hour,
The patterns made by sunlight on those ceilings,
The German band tromboning on the corner
Fading laments for Genevieve and June,
Damp smells, diplomas, cobwebs, cindered yards,
Lugubrious moustaches, high-winged collars,
Tied bundles of old newspapers and books
On esperanto, self-help, concentration,
The wastages of effort and of love.

Coughing and spitting by the radiator,
The old men listen to the wireless now
The world has turned into a coalyard where
Life which had died in shame is reborn free.
These years that saw declensions of the heart
Unguessed at on assistants' summer evenings
When ghostly skirts were whispering in the dark,
Saw also freedoms, huge across the sky
Grimy with blood and fire against which foundered

Towering gasometers, crossed girders, gantries.
Disgust itself is freedom, as is fear.
What steers us to destructions has released
Many from corridors, the servant's guile,
The clerk's reliable, deft-fingered grace,
Imperial mirrors cracked across the smile
Of duty on the dowager's creamed face.
A daily drudgery of approximate justice
Is incumbent yet upon the brave who crouch
Still over tasks upon the drumming floor.
But the eyes of survivors will ask both more and less.
And no one now need ever fear a disgrace.
The responses the night is listening to are aware
Of the irrelevant ignobility of distress.

RESPONSIBILITIES

My window shook all night in Camden Town
Where through the cutting's murk the sibilant engines
Pounded past, slowly, gasping in the rain.
Three o'clock was a distant clanking sound.

On Primrose Hill the gasfire in my room
Hissed for more money while the sofa bristled.
The unopened wardrobe stared sepulchrally.
It could have been my predecessor's tomb.

Daily I strolled through leaves to look for letters,
A half of bitter or a chance encounter.
My state was ecstasy, illusion, hunger,
And I was often lectured by my betters.

What wonder that I seldom rose till three
When light was leaking from the grimy primrose
That is the western sky of winter London,
Light in the head, lugubrious, cynical, free.

The past, implausible and profitless,
Is yet a part of us, though I suppose
Gide has the right of it: who have no sense
Of their own history know most happiness.

And yet I set that autumn sunlight down,
That delicate, pale ochre and that haze;
My eye so idle and the afternoon
So still and timeless with the haze withdrawn.

I could disown them like a thirties poet
And yet I set inexplicables down,
And scattered images of London when
With a true love I could most truly know it.

The cavernous Rowtons where the footsteps grew
Unsteadily down each corridor and passed,
The stages marked on all my bootless journeys:
A pub, a railing and a short way through.

I groped through bombsites on the Finchley Road,
Fog in the stomach, blanketed in cold.
Next morning when the gears began to groan
Whatever else I had, I had no load.

No more than when in Hammersmith one morning
The sun lit up the Broadway through the fog.
Incarnadine, transported I was stalking
Beside the early buses in that dawning.

Nightly the wagons splashed along Watling Street,
Battened down, bound for the pool or for the smoke,
Waiting for lifts I did not know myself
An avatar, a prehistoric beat.

I saw the landscape of old England like
A man upon the moon: amazing shapes,
Wheels, pulleys, engines, slag-heaps, bricks and dirt,
And furnace sunsets frowning through the smoke.

And heard the poets of old England too
In Watney's pubs repeating cricket scores
And Dylan stories, talk of our medium
And principles and programmes (radio).

The past, predestined, populous and over
Clings in the dampening leaves, the smell of petrol,
On the brown northern heights where I remember
Highgate and Hampstead in a fine October.

THE PERSUADERS

They have been with us always, the persuaders,
Public relations men for this or that,
Right from the very first: a snub-nosed playmate,
A jocular uncle with a dented hat.

The tough guys in the lavatory at school,
The companions in the scouting through the park,
The popular senior who was good at English
And prayed in chapel at the edge of dark.

The girls next door, the friend's discursive father,
The oddest ones and those who went quite straight,
The extremists who boasted how they got it,
And those who simply kept a fresh-faced date.

Some of course never made any sort of secret
Of the fine fact that they possessed a cause:
The manly masters with their tufted eyebrows,
The at least literate with their Bernard Shaws.

But many others worked more deviously:
The freckled rebel who was yet the fashion,
The normal, average guy whose eyes we liked,
The sick, squeezing remorse out of compassion.

Both those who would have us better ourselves or others
And those who said, it's daring, or, it's done;
The ones who cared, or didn't care for convention,
The ones who plugged what is, or isn't fun.

For what they called amusing, or rewarding,
For what proved your normality, or what
They thought essential to the role progressive,
You might say, for whatever you were not:

The fox that lost a tail, the fox that found one,
The member, and the man without a friend,
The grinning sinner and the smiling hero,
Finding our love of archetypes had no end,

Day in, day out kept up their deft persuasions,
Proffering an assimilable fiction,
Assuming we'd agree it was the thing.
And each said: just ignore that contradiction.

But early, early we knew what was fun,
The difference between enthusiasm and joy;
And nearly always knew them for a fraud,
For once, ye cliffs and isles, there was a boy.

And yet, and yet they were the food of growth,
A few of those experiments and fictions;
And the imitative faculty can be thanked
For certain reparatory addictions;

And if we had never learned how to pretend
We were what we were assumed by the gang to be
In some ways we'd be poorer perhaps, and sadder,
Sunk in the pride of our timidity;

And much that's not bad is partly what we grew to
Through seeing ourselves in someone else's eyes …
Of course we might have been, well, more selective,
And given a few familiars a surprise,

For apart from all the nausea and reaction,
The gradual loss of self, the knowledge of crime
Without enjoyment, there's the unredeemable
And ineffably doleful waste of time.

DUALITIES OF PRIDE

1.
Pride, that spoiled the present tense,
Stopped unpremeditated act,
And tainted with its patronage
The simpler urgings of the heart,
Permitted neither homely hope
Nor the needed miracle
Since prohibiting response
To the eyes that might expose.
Pride that spent the evening elsewhere,
Pride that refused the proffered chance,
Whose victim now will never know
What was proper at the time
Because he could not stoop to ask,
Committed to a false pretence,
Pretending he already had.
Great negative and numbing pride,
All whose converse is with ghosts,
Master servile as a slave,
Pale imprisoned governor,
Driving all desire out
Other than the secret need
To commune with enemies,
Measure the extent of pain
It has given and received,
Incessantly, insatiably
Compare the loss and failure with
Trembling confreres in the night
Old confederates of hate.

2.
Pride transmuting fear's confusions
Into a necessity
For an absolute election
Beyond the judgement of the mob,
Renewing in apparent failure
Both supremacy and pain;
Pride which passed by happiness
And made disdain a principle,
Pride the alchemy of envy,

Pride forbidding explanation,
Contemptuous alike of both
The punctual and the helpless charmers;
Pride which would not settle for
Admiring evenings in the nowhere
And equally refused the honour
Of the evenings in the somewhere
Since denying any centre,
Constructing for itself a prison.
Extortionate and sleepless pride
Perpetuating ceaselessly
The torments of its dual fate
And its abstract ecstasy,
Devising trials for itself
Beyond an enemy's devising:
Mark of destined martyrs with
No hope of crowning victory,
Ruling and anarchic saints
Who have overcome degree.

ELYSIUM

A gabled house abutting on a lane
Which leads down to the pub,
Sea-light behind.
Western stone walls, fields fading into blue.
Hills with white houses under inland sea-light.
All flares and sparkles: whitewash, granite, gorsebush.

Everyone mooches gradually to the garden
Where the first up are chatting after breakfast,
No hangovers, no clouds except for languor,
Easy intoxicants to exalt the talk.
Roses and fuchsia, box smells, gravel, trees.
A prose writer or two, a man of power
To give our stories status.
The poets equal in the sight of God.
Indulgent girls, skins diaphane with promise.

Everything trembles, nothing moves or slips,
One day in outer time,
One day in series in eternity.

The village noises still suggesting summer,
Dogs, children, hens, a single chugging boat
Prove that the after-life is actual:
Walls can be touched, found warm, and mortar crumbles.

Why not?
We've seen unlikely
Things materialise in this existence.
Surprise is a condition of our being.

NARCISSUS

What he saw was not, of course, himself
But the self who had waited her word in order to be
The one he could see when he murmured her murmur over,
The he believed in because of incredible she.

It was she who, her hair tumbling down, was gazing.
It was her lips that opened admiration.
So he saw, staring into his eyes for answer.
What he felt was her unique emotion.

Her clear regard had widened for his being
Which was his ecstasy now as he gave her a word
To describe what he – she – saw when they met in the mirror,
He being her, and she, of course, his reward.

So it was she who, her hair belled by leaning, was looking,
Dissolving into himself through the fabulous fact of her love.
Prolonging his gaze on himself, the double admirer
Joyed for them both now, he beneath and above.

And he was his hero now, as reciprocating
He saw what she saw in himself, individual
Comrade and lover; heads almost touching, his doubts
Were, as the saying goes, only residual.

And for that gaze on him he even suffers,
Baring his flesh to the cold and whatever may come,
So that he sees, Narcissus, sharing her shiver,
The risks which he takes, his acrobatic aplomb.

And plummeted down, Narcissus, through the illusion
To only a sort of calamity, way of being
Narcissus, regarder of self and adopter of beauty's
Reflective look as his own cold way of seeing.

ON A CHANGE IN LITERARY FASHION
from the Irish of Eochaidh O hEoghusa (circa 1603)

Every change is a fortune
If you look the right way at it.
A change has come upon us
Which surprises me with advantage.

My probing, hard-edged statements
I have been forced to abandon
For a sort of free poetics
Which are vastly more in fashion.

For my complicated occlusions
I earned only disgust and anger.
The majority said that my much worked
Verses were not worth unravelling.

So from now on, no matter how gifted,
I renounce pride, profit and favour,
If a single one of my verses
Looks difficult to a day labourer.

Free verse on the open road:
Since that is all that's demanded
I'll undertake to supply it
In spite of my ancient masters.

There isn't one without talent
Who will prove as loose and artless
As I in my effortless ramblings
Out here along with the rest.

And having abandoned at last
My hard, mysterious ways
I have found it a stroke of luck
They no longer earned any praise.

I share in the general loving
Through vague dishonest versing
And would earn even more affection
But for fear that the earl might listen.

But my lord and critic Tyrconnell
Having gone off to England,
Aedh's son, who liked the complex,
I need not fear his opinion.

Almost my heart used be breaking
In shaping to my satisfaction.
A way to health and leisure
Is the coming of this new fashion.

CHARACTER

They used to tell us about something they called "character".
They talked of building and developing it like Charles Atlas
about muscle,
Probably still go on about it I suppose, even after all *these*
years.
Character was what got you up quickly in the nervous
morning,
Shrinking from cold water out of the green taps at the trough,
bodies flinching and fearing, vaporizing into the crowd.
They were ambiguous about the matter of the crowd.
If you had character you conformed,
That is to say you were not an oddity, but you did not
conform too much.
You played games but did not tell dirty stories.
You stood up, but only for approved principles, not
private and probably peculiar ones of your own.
You carried a missal, but were, somehow, popular.
It helped to be a centre half.

Character polished the shoes and combed the watered hair
just like vanity did, but from different motives.
Character stood up to the bully though, come to think of it, to
achieve any dominance, even over louts, he must have had
his share of it.
Character later conferred authority at the top having got
you there.
Oddly enough it also made you content and trustworthy if
you stood with fraying cuffs at the tall desk down below.
There was a certain kind of character for clerks.
And another for their employers.
It was a vital ingredient in their relationship.
There was a knowledge that one wasn't quite the man the
other was,
But he was expected to have character when it came to
handling the other fellow's money,
Even though he got damn all for doing it.
Character also meant not fearing things,
Though you were expected to fear the law very much and
poverty too, not to mention the possibility of destitution,
And of course encouraged to fear God and the Devil both,
night and morning.

A sure mark of character and a way to build it also was self-denial,

Not having another for the road, not indulging too much in sensual pleasures and not taking what you could get,

Though I don't see that aspect of character in the sensuous, upper-class, pitiless face of the young Churchill.

I think that the ones who wore clerks' collars had actually come to believe that their betters were like themselves, an honest, sober and sexually restrained lot,

Otherwise they would not have had so much fear of disgrace – not just of being punished but of whatever it was being known –

And were stupid enough to think that the code they observed applied to their lords as well as their masters.

They should have known that the dog who eats the other dogs in the end is generally a gay dog all round.

With appetites.

Take Sir Douglas Haig here now in the coloured supplement.

The notion of character began to decline after his war somehow,

Being at its height I suppose in nineteen fourteen,

But he has obvious character,

Boots, belts, set of the cap, grasp of the cane.

Even this poor devil Plumer here beside him with his belly bulging out of his uniform who has come to the comic caricature stage of character,

Even he is sort of intimidating,

As well he might be.

Someone else, though, must have polished Sir Douglas's boots for him,

Someone to whom let's hope he afterwards gave a good character.

He'd polished boots for others of course years ago when he'd fagged,

And surely he licked a few pairs on his way up the ladder.

The ability to make decisions like generals are supposed to have was a part of character.

I wonder, though, were those moustaches coming down like that over the mouths,

Were they in case the latter organs revealed subtly, softly, somehow a certain lack of character,

And what about the big decision makers like Hitler, who with his nerves absolutely banjaxed from strychnine, mercury and other hoop-las could still make the decision to destroy all Germany wall by wall?

And me thinking that when my nerves are a bit cut up from drink I can't make decisions at all.

And G. told me about ski-ing to keep fit because he has decisions to make every day in the course of business.

We must be talking about making the wrong decisions.

If it means nothing to you to destroy the world finally and forever it can't be too difficult to do it – even if your face has gone green and one leg is paralysed from the mad doctor's drugs.

The good characters who have character are rather left behind by the Genghis Khans when it comes to making the big decisions.

When it comes to making decisions Hitler showed a load of character.

He started a lot of consequences.

Let's get the show on the road.

Get the big wagons rolling.

Character was also related to a certain kind of energy,
The dogged effort kind.
Take literature for example.
Them Victorian bores, writing five thousand words every day
    before breakfast,
They had character.
Of course telling the truth, owning up, that was supposed to
    show character also:
They didn't bother much about telling the truth, in some
    respects anyway.
I've owned up in print in my time to a few comic and curious
    things.
That must show character.
Of course nobody asked me to,
Then too the writers of the reign of Queen Victoria were great
    fellows for character,
You know, like Micawber.
The differences between one man and another, clothes and
    class and height and hump,
Nearly always to do with success or failure, accent and
    occupation,
That was what made characters.

We don't set much store by that kind of thing nowadays I
   hope.
We're all much the same in the burrow.

Somehow, somewhere, for some of us, the whole business of
   character went wrong.
Something sordid got into it.
Shall I say, unsympathetic?
Something stupid and boring that thought boredom and
   ugliness were virtues,
Putting its head under the cold water while the bodies came
   awake at the trough.
And though it's not nice not to have much character,
And if you like your friends and even your forbears at all it
   involves you in a lot of unpleasant remorse
(The gay dogs with the strong characters who become prime
   ministers don't suffer much of that)
It's better, I'm convinced,
And life, is, after all, a choice between evils –
I mean it's awful to have no job
But it would be worse to have one –
It's probably better to have no character,
Or even to be a bad character,
Or a weak character
Than to be eaten up with character
Which after all is no good for anything but success,
Or conformity,
Or salvation
Or destruction,
Or not being – in certain ways only mind you, after all there's
   more than one kind of burden –
A burden to others,
Things I don't personally set much store by
Since they seem to drive out nicer things like
Idleness,
Contemplation,
Absorption of images,
An occasional creative outbreak
And long idle sessions among families of friends.
And since the sort of understanding and compassion for the
   weak that I think to be perhaps the most important thing
   of all

(And the weak we'll have always with us)
Is only to be found among those who are weak themselves,
   though perhaps something else as well –
I mean it's all very well in theory for Kipling to talk about
   needing no aid from men that he might help such men as
   need but I've never met one like that, snotty bastards mostly
   who think the just man is touched twenty times a day –
There's an end of argument.
Though, mind you, when it comes to stoicism of a sort,
And stubbornness of a sort,
And energy of a sort,
I've got plenty.
And I can take plenty of punishment
And still come out fighting
Or loving.
To enjoy the physical world of one's walks one has to be on
   holidays.
And the enjoyment of sunlight is acute when the holidays are
   earned.
And also acute when they're happily stolen.
One way or another I'm on my holliers a good deal of the
   time.

BLESSED ARE THE POOR IN SPIRIT

Tortured with honour,
Sloughing it off,
Tortured with honesty,
Sloughing it off,
Hating the sound of
Apology's cough,
Blaming myselfhood
More often than not,
Knowing myself like
The kettle the pot,
Meaning myself when
I sweat, stop the rot

I see those who are not honest travelling unconcerned
(More, in many cases, luck to them)
I see those who are not honourable going about unperturbed
(More, in many particular instances, power to them)
And there are millions who don't know themselves from
    Adam (which would be cause enough for annoyance even if
    they weren't bores or moralists for the most part, in verse or
    worse),
The quick ones taking advantage of others' complexity,
The driven by greed and avarice marching in the sodality,
The provincial snobs to whom you couldn't conceivably
    explain the social hierarchy and what levels you and they
    operated on without teaching them the language in which
    you weren't bothering to insult them,
And though God knows even unconscious hypocrisy must be
    horrible beneath the clothes
If they're oblivious that's the way it is and I suppose this even
    applies
To some on benches.
Praising the rascal in rambunctious verses while sentencing
    tinkers for stealing bags of wet turf.

But I see too a more comic level of deception which can
    hardly be other than deliberate,
The big, High Tory, Buchan and Billingsgate, boy scout and
    buggery swizz.
Between the Churchill fortunes founded on a whore
And the successive centuries of preachment about honour,
    courage, virtue,

Between Thackeray's activities in the brothel
And the misses admired in the books which led many down
lanes,
Between the goings on at the top as the limousines glide on
and off the telly, black doors open and close, the bowlers
pause on the steps and through the rear side windows we
can see departing profiles grave with necessity
And the high chorus from the same quarter which has never
stopped through centuries of mutual trickery and public
and private slaughter,
There is a class of a gap which is worse than comic,
Though it is that.

Seeing all this
(And even believing there are those who may be mentally and
morally honest all the way down the line and as honourable
as the day is long,
Decent folk who do no wrong,
Though not enquiring into their mental capacity,
Great men included,
Still less into how much they limit their responsibility,
Since I limit my own)

Seeing the rest
And being, more or less,
Tortured with honour,
Sloughing it off,
Tortured with honesty,
Sloughing it off,
Hating the sound of
Apology's cough,
Blaming myselfhood
More often than not,
Knowing myself like
The kettle the pot,
Meaning myself when
I sweat, stop the rot

I should try to convince myself, even at three o'clock in the
morning,
That I'm not altogether as wretched, worthless and dishonest
a fellow as I feel.

WAR POEM

Valerian, a local flower,
Likes Wellington and Waterloo.
The Irish marched to any drum
From Spion Kop to Fontenoy.
When Collins' bullets pocked the dome
I wasn't in a State to know.
In thirty-two as well as Dev
Came large campaigns in Manchukuo,
We fought it out in slush beside
The asylum where the Slaney flows.
Jim Lynch and I were Japanese
When not swamped in the Gran Chaco.
The age of lead and cut-outs passed
And Baillie-Stuart marched no more
(What Sandhurst bugles in our blood
And what blood-thirsty mites we were).
Ras Kassa though as tall as spears
Was no match for Badoglio.
Came Spain and Jim, a restive spirit,
Wrote to Quiepo de Llano,
He wanted in on any side
In any sort of real war.
He joined the blue-shirts, then, being baulked,
The I.R.A., he had a go
At length high in the German skies.
I heaved a neutralist heigh-ho
And dithered where Valerian
Commanded heights round Waterloo.
There's something in what Johnson said
And no reportage of the bo–
Ring aspects of it quite suffice
To compensate for a lost war.
Whatever reason said because
I won no wounds I bore a scar.
Nor could the staring facts root out
Such strange ambitions, even girls'
Indifference to uniforms,
Remove the masochistic, ro–
Mantic censored rubbish from
My screens and make them fit to view

Until much hoarier than I was
In Autumn nineteen forty-four.
And this applies to other things,
Like Scott I pined for ever more
Evidence from other worlds,
Enjoyed my own scenario
Of courtship and of self-escape,
The rescues and the racing cars,
Although I'm rescueless to date
And never hammered round Le Mans,
Nor ever either won the fight,
Having climbed up off the floor,
Alas, alack! This sedentary
Trade it's not only Yeats it broke.
But yet compared to most it's not
All that much lacking in rough sport,
And what the hell, intensity
Has not been wanting, danger nor
A casualty rate among
My lot of about one in four,
Whatever about self-esteem.
Or in some darling's eyes a glow.
Of course it's said all round today
The civilized don't hanker for
The epaulettes, the smart salutes,
The laurels round the soldier's brow,
Jabbing with bayonets, dropping bombs
On children, women and the old.
Militarist is a dirty word.
If bombing babies is supposed
This last time to have been quite just
In part at least that is because
No one could otherwise have had
That great experience, a good war;
And those who had one couldn't come
On TV or the radio
And in the tones of warriors say
That war is frightful don't you know.
In fact now that I think of it
It's so unfashionable to
Confess to ever having had
Such military hankerings or

Confusions about proving one's
Manhood in the sphere of mars
(Though I think much of what I felt
In the aforesaid forty-four
Was probably the product of
Unceasing propaganda for
Provence's propertied ethos shrunk
Transformed to Hollywood machismo)
I'd better cut it out and give
Myself more marks for moral fore–
Sight, thinking warlike thoughts but watching,
On sunny afternoons of woe,
Valerian, that local flower,
Take root on walls round Waterloo.

THE ELEPHANT TO THE GIRL IN BERTRAM MILLS' CIRCUS

I, like a slow, morose and shabby fatalist,
Unfitted for presumption, trousers too loose,
Shamble towards you, scented, delicate,
Your eyes glittering myopically back at the front rows,
Shoulder blades bared to me,
Imagining, although I cannot see
Your faintly trembling lips, white teeth, those fixed bright
   eyes,
Your desperate smile and stare.
I stoop, mournful that this should be
Over your lacquered hair,
My soft tongue touches it,
My loose pink lips enclose
Your closing eyes and nose,
Between the inside of your thighs
And the front rows' avid gaze
I drop my trunk.
Then you lean back, breasts taut
And grip my ears,
Abandoned to decision now you raise
Your legs and close them round my forehead bone
And we proceed on circuit, we alone,
You in my dark, my gravity, my space
Waiting for your release.
You are my victim, yes, but all my care,
Your face invisible and your shining hair
Within my mouth's pink softness,
My foul breath
Your fierce preoccupation.
The rest possess
Only your white long arms and legs,
Your backside's elevation
And whatever consolation
Lies in the fact that they can watch our progress
Yet when I set
Gently your beautiful buttocks down again
And, lifting lip and trunk, reveal your face,
Your smile, your hair in place,
Only a slight

Worry about mucus mingles with your response
To them and their applause.
And when you twist and show on solid ground
Around the ring to all of them the tight
Behind and breasts which I have carried round,
And doing so invite
With effulgent wave and kiss
Them all to re-possess
The high-heeled girl that lately ran such risk –
I am the loser for my tenderness.

OBLIGATIONS

Claudius murdered his wife,
Nero, his mother:
Commodus also his trouble and strife,
Caracalla, his brother.

By the Emperors, whom nothing outside themselves could
    hinder,
These cuttings away were practised
Almost as a rule.
To have borne with the inconveniences attached to having
    kindred?
Their Imperial Majesties?
Do you take a God for a Fool?

So you who in some thin-walled suburb endure
Swollen ankled mother,
Cantankerous wife,
Perhaps even ne'er-do-well brother,
And daughters who have somehow ceased to be pure:
Do not say, it is every man's duty, the natural law, a law of
    life.
The Emperors, who were free, knew no such obligations.
Say: I am loyal, or stupid, or self indulgent, or, I don't like
    strife.
Say: it is in obedience to the Christian revelations.
Troubled though you may be by ungrateful laughter,
Believe you'll receive your reward in the subtle hereafter.

Or say: whatever they may have considered themselves free
    from or above,
Those bloody Emperors knew nothing about love.

ENQUIRERS

Retreating as best I may
Towards the watershed of the traffic,
Defences in disarray,
Gaze balancing on a gull
At a busy corner,
All passing girls lost to the eye,
I lie to the enquirer.
So much for the morning.
A day's work behind them later,
The pub established as base,
Bottled supplies secured,
The attackers resume the advance.
What are you doing now?
How are things with you?
Are you working on anything new?
Casually concerned,
Indifferently curious
Or malevolent and sly
On the slacks and jumper occasions
As well as in uniform
They probe to the heart of one's matters,
One's justifications.
Behind them the suburbs lie
From which they can conjure up
Flocks of newspaper notions
About tax-dodging authors,
Love-affairs, divorces,
Reinforcements
In hazy battalions.
Nothing in my circumstances
Could conceivably satisfy.

SUMMER POEM: IRELAND

As lately as ten days ago
The lifted chestnut candles
Swayed in unburdened air.
The ash leaves, last to come, had still
The amber red of the gum.
Under a bursting sun
The young grass was burnished:
You could distinguish in the green
Many degrees of bronze and shades of brown,
Blue sky and a sea-breeze blowing for days.
On the side of the sky away from the sun
The blue had a blow-hole of white,
An opacity,
Or a translucence,
A suggestion of other light.
Lilac, laburnum, acacia, currant,
Coloured and domestic bushes,
Reconciled all the Victorian houses.
My hut in the garden where I could work
Smelled of wood and creosote
Like huts one time at the seaside.

Now after ten days rain
The candles are stripped to their stalks.
Steamy as Vietnam
Ireland suspires under cloud.
The national colours, green and grey,
Shine eerily from earth and sky.
De Valera, the old wet blanket,
Is back in his damp park.
"Soft day, your honour."
The monsoon breaks
And I am broke.
There is something in lost wet summers
That symbolizes our fate,
However fallacious the pathos.
Red roses and fuchsia flower.
The one holds in wet softness,
The other lets slip the drop,
In their red a suggestion of black.

We remember other summers
Under an Irish sky.
"It can't be healthy – Look at all that green,"
Said Clay.

AT THE ZOO

My sense of justice is constantly offended.
The disgustingly sleek seals have a little landscaped park
And what is practically a lake to show off in.
The dull old hippos only a small hot yard and a muddy pool.
Doubtless my feeling that this is wrong is a product of my
    ignorance.
I know nothing about the hippopotamus's real needs.
But I do note that the seals are performers and appear to be
    popular
With the general public.

I read the neatly presented information on the fences.
It is mostly about the important question of the role of male
    and female.
There is of course a lot of variation but it seems to me at least
That in the wild state anyway the males get the worst of it,
    condemned
To a curious sort of aloneness, always on their guard, fighting,
Cut off from the innocent young and cosy domesticity.
And though the males that have numbers of nubile,
    presumably eager-to-please females as harems do indeed do
    well,
Where would I ever have been if only one male was going to
    be chosen?
At least by success in personal combat and not by a secret
    ballot of the possible seraglio?

It says about polar bears that the only time male and female
    polar bears come together
Is for the brief mating season, usually April.
But this is July and there are two cooped up together in this
    grim, grey grotto
Like a background to a Mantegna crucifixion.
One looks to my untutored eye like a male, the other a female.
So what is this? Marriage?
According to the notice it is highly unnatural
And unless this particular pair have evolved (become
    resigned) in captivity
It is obviously cruel, whoever is responsible.

I reflect that wild is scarcely the word for these wild animals.
They do not attack the bars, do not hurl themselves at the
     netting.
The more dangerous the beast, the more retiring he seems
And the gladder of the pen that separates him from us.
Their self-control in the heat amazes me,
And the self-effacement of the more bodeful and serious
     among them, not clowns or performers:
Bar-dappled, leaf-dappled, camouflaged where possible,
None playing the hero, crying
Give me liberty or give me death.

After two hours the children's enthusiasm is almost unabated,
But there is something about these glassy-eyed wild animals
That is too remote for my taste.
It may be the lack of facial expression, the constant yawning,
But I'm afraid that the animal empathy poem is another kind
     that I'll just have to stay guilty about.

And when we get to the disorderly bus queue I gladly turn
     my attention
To the members of my own species, particularly the females
     of mating age
Of whom there are many present in various states of summer
     undress.
In spite of the fact that some of them are chewing bubble gum
     and carrying transistors
From which come the most inane of our human sounds, the
     voices of popular performers
Who could doubtless cause most to swoon by appearing in
     person and would not have to put on half the performance I
     would have to put on to make amorous headway,
My response is interest and approval, even, in one case,
     something like passion,
Though of course where my own passionate or animal
     instincts are concerned
I am all too conscious of the obstacles, not crying either
Give me liberty or give me death.

TO CERTAIN AUTHORS

Although our lovely and laborious art
Is lumped in with performances like yours,
And one or two who ride our horse are praised
Along with those who tumble in a cart
To catch whatever's coming from the boors,
And even by froth of gossiping are raised
To fame like yours, although of course not paid,
Do not think that the rest of us must smart
With envy, waiting in vain outside those doors.
Ours was the option, ours the choice we made,
And ours a different, no less just reward.

TO SILENCE THE ENVY IN MY THOUGHT

Those I have known walk bravely on the platforms,
Loudspeakers bang their words off Clery's wall.
The words are hoarse, befitting the loudspeakers,
And the long, tired other nights in the fight for the cause.
I learn from the papers precisely how they function:
This one is fuelled on power, that one on the poor,
They draw from public attention the same kind of sustenance
That held up the head of the head, the elected boy.

It must be passing brave to be a Prince
And ride in triumph through Persepolis.

O I can imagine it too, have had my leanings towards
    speaking,
Can see myself in my greatness standing foursquare,
Walking and talking with others equally eminent,
A so many years old memory to the poor;
Coming in for a while and loyally serving another,
Remaining the legendary one who was loved above all,
The man in the gap who came to the radio station
And told them the best and the worst with a breaking voice.

But one of the differences is – unfortunately there are so many –
That my imagination leaps to the end of the road,
Forgetting, honest to god, like Coriolanus,
Precisely the sort of indignity that is involved.

And not only that but the sort of ridiculous detail,
Not like the dandelion leaves of my walkaday world:
The Collins and Danton stimulants for the sad spirit
Have little to do with the case of these vote-getting clerks.
And where is the action except in my future of cities,
My world beyond steps where the columns link still in the
    sun?
If this is the height of it, here in the street before Clery's,
There isn't much poetry in it, nor in it for poets.

And if it is so, though I doubt it, that this body's feelings
At work on the digits, the totals, the pensions per cent
Can accelerate change so much that it humanly matters

Or produce a significant change in the spirit of man –
I admit to myself that he has the more energy for it,
More competence, cunning and method, I'm sure for the best.

And the spirit will change as the sunlight falls sideways this
    autumn
And the tufts of the grass turn golden and brick grips the sun,
While garden and gate-lodge and paddock hold still in
    September
And tomatoes exude for the last time geranium smells.
More likely the change if I stick to my last in the autumn.
Commune with your heart on your bed said the psalmist be
    still.

LUNCHTIME TABLE, DAVY BYRNE'S

The prawns accomplished now he forks into the steak
And kidney pie (a different proposition)
Laps at his ale and looks, his anecdote
A munch or two behind, about the table.
All here possess the teanga, Times's, jobs
In Academe, Departments, Bords and Comhluchts.
A name is recognised, stools shift, expected
Laughter of wits about the well-known wags
Their backsides to a liberal overlap
For liberal opinions round the board.
Behold inheritors.
For them the grey geese spread
Etcetera and Paudeen in damp grass
Stared up at four-cloaked prophets on a hill
Promising nation states, proprietors,
Communes and comfort, final freedom from
The caubeen and the caub, the cold potato so
That the wise Gaelic could flow free again
And ecumenical Dominicans absolve
And Beckett follow Joyce to give a cachet
To jobs concerned with handouts, trade and art.
The tweed ties prove it and the tourist board,
The scholar-critic from beyond the seas –
O'Casey is his field and Con his contact.

Far from the lunchtime table where the Beltra
Spews the bog water to Atlantic waves
Paudeen still waits. But they have him at heart:
A list of liberal causes and the language,
Vatican Two and some suburban sex.
Back to the office then, bilingual.
After that home and in again to Godot.
Beyond that, nationhood, and further still,
Pensioned, unjobbed, confront eternity.
Walling the west still falls Belmullet rain.
Ink over Blacksod ebony clouds begin.

LETTER TO AN ENGLISHMAN
(1975, PUBLISHED 1983)

I send you greetings from south-western Clare,
A bleak, cropped place, inhospitably bare,
The limestone having given out at Ennis
And brought stone walls and fuchsia to a finis,
Not to mention trees, which, in the Atlantic wind
Will scarcely grip, or, if they do grip, bend:
Which doesn't, though, I should say straight away
Mean that I'm now a cottage industry,
The writer on a headland in sea boots,
Nurturing or re-discovering his roots,
Guessing at fishermen's psychology
And making a pig's breakfast of the sea.
No, my penchant for the odd in ambience,
The unorthodox, the baw-ways circumstance,
The chapter of, well, accidents has me
In a place you haven't heard of, called Kilkee,
A watering place in winter like a set
For some bad movie where the lovers (wet)
Can walk along the cliffs and bid farewell
Beside the bandstand while the long sea swell
Washes the credits off, a seaside place
Which summer touched for some, let's hope, with grace:
Parents who watching antics with a smile
Knew troubles wouldn't grow up for a while,
Little ones scooping, architecting castles,
Grave girls who came to be, and were, unfastened,
And, hot with premonition, found out more
Or less what others had a year before.
Yes, in winter, though it's more than slightly *outré*,
This painted, put down by the shore Kilkee,
There's matter for reflection and some history
To brood on; for instance Charlotte Brontë
Came here on honeymoon: unhappily
Her ever-after lasted but a year,
A thought in which there isn't too much cheer,
So let's remember Tennyson instead
Who, being A. De Vere's guest, upped and fled
To this last lonely spot where inspiration
Came in the guise of utter desolation,
Producing that strange poem, "Break, break, break ..."
The best he ever wrote for old sake's sake.
And fairly cheerful too is the thought, I think,

Of Percy French, who whipped out pen and ink
One day upon the esplanade and wrote
(At least the locals say he did and quote
The lot to prove it) that nice piece about
The West Clare Railway, or, if something more
Is needed to associate this curved shore
With literature, there's Emily Lawless who
Dived from the cliffs into enclosing blue,
Shocking the onlookers with her bravery,
A tall and straight-backed goddess of the sea.
There's even a resident poet, Liddy, that
You met one time in Dwyer's of Leeson Street.
You may remember him as *outrecuidant*
And I must confess I'd rather, when I go
Up the cliff path see Tennyson above me,
Standing at gaze, or, either, Charlotte Prunty
Come downward hand in hand and tête-à-tête
With hubby, Arthur Nicholls, and her fate.
Yes, history, a finished matter, lets us
Contemplate much that, met with, might distress us.
I read the Reverend Bagwell's "Ireland Under
The Tudors" which records a deal of horror,
Famine and pestilence, grief, greed and slaughter.
He gives some meaning to the ruined structures,
Yeats's ambiguous symbols, keeps and castles,
Lined out along the Shannon where the Earl
Of Desmond's harriers hung many a churl,
Where Raleigh rode with Spenser while the province
Starved at their horse's heels: conquistadores,
Adventurers, courtiers, gents, or jacks-in-office,
Some even said, defenders of all freemen
From reaction and the Spanish Inquisition.
It was in fact not very far from here
That the great ships in morning light appeared,
Reeling like giants off this shale-bound shore,
Artefacts bigger than anything seen before,
Their sails like ragged clouds, their cabins castles,
Strange portents of a world already vanished.
Monstrous they were, but man-made, those great ships
And manned by desperate humans with parched lips.
You see I've read your letter well and am
Working around to answer like a ram

Wrestling with an intractable opponent,
Going round in circles but still quite determined:
A rural image, let's hope it is authentic,
But who could say, except a rural critic?
Strange, though we've rural poets here galore
We don't have rural critics to keep score.
Leastways I'm glad you're interested in our history,
Which, as you say, is still to most a mystery,
But gladly though I welcome such an interest,
In this here briary island's past,
The fact is, my dear fellow, it won't last.
Though every time the shooting and the bombing
Start up again Hibernophiles go thumbing
Through standard histories hopefully re-issued
Or brighter tomes which have been just commissioned
From instant experts who, quite rightly, think
When blood is spilled, one should likewise spill ink,
And that to have a London publisher
Is, for a college lecturer, cause for rapture,
The remainder men will shortly have their share
Of books by Dudley Edwards and De Paor,
The reason being that no-one likes a story
Which keeps on coming round to the same gory
Sequence of crimes and offers no denouement.
No-one can stand a yarn which won't move onward.
But Ireland's history like Mr Yeats's
Returning gyres is really sort of stasis.
Here in the south of course we have some progress,
A rather spotty sort with many setbacks
And huge distorting factors, psychological
And otherwise. I'd say the post-colonial
Era in southern Ireland's a success.
I mean we have a post-colonial mess
Aggravated by uncertainty as to whether
The colony is really off the tether
(Another rural image. Soon I'll set up
As a rival to them all and never let up).
Well anyway we safeguard all investments,
Both home and foreign, pay back money lent us
And export raw materials, food and labour,
Mostly to our post-imperial neighbour.
We also have what's now called a two party

– Both of them much the same – democracy.
Ruled by themselves, yclept Majority,
Most can sleep sound at nights, this side the border,
And have free speech, Jack Lynch and law and order.
The world progresses, as the liberals said
In English history books, of course it would,
With freedom broadening down from precedents
The Mother Of All Other Parliaments
Established, of which up in Leinster House
We have an imitation, modelled close
Enough to keep things very much the same
If most of us agree to play the game.
We also have our social welfare laws
Combined with modified free enterprise:
The present old age pension's seventy-three
Shillings a week, with TV licence free.
I know it's wrong to be dissatisfied.
This system is the best that's been devised
For those more fortunate, the ones who've got
A job, a concrete house, a little plot
At back and front, a car parked in the garage
And don't want visions, ructions or catharsis,
Content between the cradle and the grave,
To cradle others, pray and re-pay and save.
And since the local bourgeois revolution,
The one we had, albeit an Irish version,
That is a realisable ambition
For those who were born or educated towards it,
If educate you care, or choose, to call it,
The process of the job examination.
They've flocked from rural Ireland into Dublin
To taste the sweets of bourgeois victory
Over the Anglo aristocracy
(For bourgeois here read also *feirmeoirí*
Which you can look up in your dictionary)
And every previous system on this planet.
They're comfy and they've got some shining gadgets.
The bourgeois revolution's a success
For many, many thanks to Patrick Pearse
And all the later clerks and petty savants,
Farmers and shopkeepers who beat the raj.
Of course it's clear from looking at the scene

With eyes I hope not specially green.
There are more glittering prizes for a few
Ordinary chaps, not unlike me and you,
But gifted with more of something: cash, acumen,
Energy, greed or even knowledge of human
Nature, a little business sense or money
Inherited from Daddy or from Mummy.
Though really I think none of these things matter
Compared to something some got on a platter,
For best of all has been since the foundation
Of this our state, a stake in revolution,
Acquired by a direct participation,
Or inherited by the second generation.
Of course they didn't calculate like that,
The ones who brought the victory about
And in the middle of the little spat
Which brought it all to pass, with brothers dying
And patriotic words and bullets flying,
Whenever there was leisure to reflect
On hunger-strike or lecture tour, dissect
The motive for it all, they didn't say
"When this is over and we have our way
We'll be the new ascendancy, we'll own
The whole bang lot, from Toe Head to Tyrone"
The ones who fought the War of Independence
Did so, and let's admit it in all fairness,
Out of the purest motives, with no thought
Of how the thing eventually would turn out,
Of how the banks, insurance, brokerage, commerce
Would fall to them. The dialectical process
Is to blame. They couldn't know the bourgeois
Revolution would be a bonanza.
They hadn't read their Marx and couldn't see
How sweet would be the sweets of victory.
They still may think that it was due to merit
And character, to hard work and sheer effort.
Aided of course by the odd little threat
And bit of blackmail, that the boys who bet
The Tans should get the jobs, the briefs, the banks
And, suddenly elevated from the ranks
Of revolution, should by freak of chance
Turn out fair dabs at very high finance.

They fought, as they thought, to make Ireland free,
Meaning their talents and their energy
Demanded outlets which they hadn't got
In the old set up from the British lot.
They wanted mostly native politics
Instead of having all run by the Brits,
Politics, the great passion of our time,
Tenacious plant which grows in every clime,
Will out like murder, but, like murder too,
However it may seem to me and you
Is seldom motiveless: *Cherchez la femme*
They say, look also for the econom–
Ic motive of political upheaval
Which makes it more indigenous and enjoyable.
And politics meant, if not control, cahoots
With bankers, manufactory of boots
Behind obliging tariff walls, "If Bob's
Your flipping uncle then the job's
Awaiting, we all know he did his bit,
His sister's son must be rewarded for it."
So the bourgeoisie down here got much of what
It wanted, one could sadly say, the lot.
What was lacking in a nation once again
Could be ignored, or glossed, or just forgotten
Until it raised again its croppy's head
And recited all the names of all the dead.
If it was partial, not a *bouleversement*,
But only a transfer, a drastic shake-up,
With fundamental structures left intact,
In their eyes it was none the worse for that.
The British system and the rule of law
With everybody free to jaw and jaw
Is better than bayonets where the basic right
To property is concerned, and our lot sought
Anxiously to preserve that simple thing.
They'd got the land. They now would have their fling
In all the ways emergent bourgeoisies
Have some right to expect. Bureaucracy
And commerce taking in each other's washing
Is more or less the formula agreed on.
Unfortunately though, "The Irish Question"
Remains, for in the Treaty "Settlement",

A Welshman, Taffy thief, to wit Lloyd George
Avoided Britain having to disgorge
Six awkward counties in the north-east corner
Round which are now a quite ridiculous border,
Where once upon a time she had sown thick
Planters who were quite alien to Mick
And his beliefs, a Calvinistic horde
Who had a hot line to a vengeful lord,
(And really of all fates that can befall
A folk the one that's clearly worst of all
Is having the Supreme Being on your side,
A chap who, after all, was crucified,
The most fervent peoples find, however sadly,
That the Deity's a very doubtful ally)
Who were brought over at the time we spoke of
When the great ships were thronging the rough ocean
And it was thought the stupid Papish Irish
Might prefer instead of Liberty of Conscience
The notions that they had themselves. Supplant them,
Said Spenser and some others, so the ranting
And as they're thought in these parts, canting Knoxians
Were brought across from bonny lowland Scotland.
And given land and made into a bastion
To keep the king safe from the Whore of Babylon.
(They didn't quite supplant them altogether.
There were natives in the bog and in the heather,
Papishes at the end of every lane,
All corresponding with the Queen of Spain.)
Of course they weren't quite homogenous.
Within the north as is there's class on class,
Atop, the Church of Ireland landed gents,
A clever breed with military bents,
Montgomerys, Alexanders, Brookes, a lot,
Whose trade is war and holding what they've got;
The business Prods, now banjaxed, but bequeathing,
Like empty staring windows in mill buildings
A legacy of anachronistic hate,
Which once they thanked their God they could create,
Hate which confirms a practical advantage,
The introjection into half the work force
Of a poison which destroys all combination
And makes them grateful for their situation,

What's called religion, freedom, British laws,
Being really jobs, advantage, indoor loos,
A recipe for racial terror stalking,
Well, let us say, self-satisfiedly walking
On the other breed, whose place is to be under
With shrilling fife and twirling drummer's thunder.
Of course the underdogs have classes too,
Some dogs mount high enough to see the view,
So there's the Papish middle class with less
Access to power, office, influence.
Than the other; as we saw before a dangerous
Denial in this democratic era,
The panacea of free politics,
The twentieth century's great drug and fix.
Anyway every Tague's in some way thwarted
Or worse, and they won't any longer stand for it.
As time goes by, though, we may see dissension
Between the ones who merely want advancement,
Whose equality or dignity's denied
Who feel some sort of insult to their pride,
I mean the northern Catholic middle classes,
And those who cling to the edge of all our abysses
Supposed to be content with bread and circuses.
The former's hope is called an aspiration
And the world has practised its accommodation.
The other's ... ? Well, who knows when sleepers wake
What they will want and even try to take?
The people of Turf Lodge and Andytown
May not be bought off with a nationalist bone.
Before all this is over they may reckon
What happened in the south, the hairy bacon
And watery soup of W.T.'s depression
(For W.T. see Edwards and De Paor
I can't explain it all to you I fear)
The grudging doles and hand-outs of the decades
Since independence weren't worth the shedding
Of blood and tears, an outcome surely that
Those who could mend things now will then regret,
Particularly those who want a stable
Ireland athwart the seaways, not a Cuba.
Instead of acting as a catalyst
You've been the opposite, whatever that is,

An agent to prevent our history happening,
Thesis, antithesis, in our case *verboten*,
The dialectic working its design
Through holy opposition, thwart and tine.
In that respect and others things were static
Hereabouts. Perhaps it's symptomatic
That what your critics always want from Ireland
Is that it should continue out-of-time land.
Old Yeats supplied a timeless twilight zone
To comfort the time-conscious of the *Fin*
De Siecle; and of late our "tribal conflict"
Has had its charms, being practically pre-historic,
Primordial, primal, primitive, all that guff
And thus good meaty strong poetic stuff,
A change from your librarian in Hull
Whose non-life was becoming rather dull.
History, Joyce said, was a nightmare from
Which he was trying to awake, but I'm
Convinced that what we suffer from round here
Is not true history, say rather fear
Of history let loose and happening.
If you're the referee then where's the ring?
Yes, history's an evil but the truth
Is that it must be lived through, like one's youth.
Like youth it's not a terminal disease.
In the long or short run it will cure itself.
But we must still confront the dreary steeples
And Catholic parliaments for chaste, pure peoples.
The cul-de-sac of nationalist politics
And the recurrence of that dismal fix–
Ation which has long obsessed the best
(As well, admittedly, as a few worst)
How to get rid of Albion and be free
From glen to glen and sea to tumbling sea
Without a definition of just what
Such freedom is and who it's going to profit:
That, I'm afraid does not amount to history,
Great rampant, rearing, pawing from the knee.
Perennial risorgimento's not
Perpetual revolution and, in fact,
The thing to which it bears the most resemblance
Is a perpetual pimply adolescence.

To change the metaphor, which is my privilege,
Old-fashioned, nationalist risorgimentos
Which come unstuck or are coffined up too early
Are like that Frankenstein's pale Weary Willie
Who was dead but didn't know it and would walk
Abroad, a stinking mummy, in the dark;
And bitter covenants of sole election
Which guaranteed a twitching god's protection,
The elect in holy frenzy clinging fast
To the wormwood ark which saved them in the past,
Entitling them to be the *herrenvolk*
And stamp on the heretical other bloke
Are not like intellectual conservatism,
A creed for Davie, Hill, Heath-Stubbs or Sisson.
Our history's murderous but also static
The worst of all worlds from the temporal viewpoint.
Returning gyres is right, we're in a lock
Like a neurotic with volition block,
Thus not the sort that could rejoice the heart
Of a conservative worth half his salt.
There's no-one can seek peace in his own ground
And praise creation for such mercies found,
While sun and lichen bind the stone together
Old values hold and still holds still the weather.
No, what we've got is bitter fruit for all.
And plucked from barbed wire, not a well-loved wall.
The lock so long considerately provided
By the dear guardian island here beside us
Has as a consequence that the states we get in
Are neither fish, flesh, fowl nor good red herring.
There's never been a stable time, a stasis
On which the true conservative could fix his
Sense of what's best, not even one to mourn for
Symbolised by a broken king at nightfall;
And the new martyrdom of modern man
Which the French started with their revolution,
That glorious martyrdom of discontent
Has hardly begun in these parts even yet.
I know we have the politics of promise.
I know there is a little economics.
I know I said the southern middle classes
Had got a toehold in what elsewhere passes

For the normal state of western man;
And it is true that out in Ballymun
People have problems which are not a whole lot
Different from those they have in Bishop's Stortford.
In Stoneybatter as in Stoke-on-Trent
You try to keep a job and pay the rent.
But when Risorgimento walks abroad
The real problems still go by the board.
Go north, come south, the primary fixation
Is still the hypothesis of the Irish nation,
Where else but here could controversy, hate
Attend the concept of the nation state?
What in France was settled under Louis Quatorze
Still fills the local correspondence columns.
We've been in tutelage since before the Spaniards
Gazed at these cliffs, their hands on useless poniards.
I won't enquire into the guardian's profits.
The usual plaint of course is that he robbed us.
But just as tragic from the victim's viewpoint
Has been the inhibition of development,
The natural flow of history and the mix
Doing its turnabouts and party tricks.
We are exhorted much, but oftenest we
Are told, don't think about your history.
The truth is that we haven't had one yet
And what you haven't had you can't forget.
Its time I ended. There's a heavy sea
Banging away there at the cliffs below me
And Emily Lawless's little Corca Bascinn's
Well salted by the spray from the Atlantic.
The waves are leaping up at George's Head.
The shale-based turf is springy to the tread
On this short day. I'll go and walk a bit
Before the winter sun, a thin bright plate
With water dripping from it goes and night
Works westward, night in Tullamore and Cahir
Succeeded by uncaring night in Clare.

RETURN THOUGHTS

I crossed from Liverpool,
The lights
Pooled on the dark water,
Walls
Swinging away,
To lay your ghost before you died.
The last of two few crossings
… little comfort
You,
Remembering and breathing
Propped on your pillows with the spring outside.

Spring '61
And down Drumcondra Road
The wind blew back the litter and the dust
Enormous chestnuts tossed
By institution walls,
Nowhere else on earth
Such green under cornflower blue.
Here too I'd been disgraced.
I wondered what dying cost.
There were doors I had to dodge.
Cloud shadows raced my thoughts.

I had not given much towards cost of living
(Except in the wrong sense)
And only half believed
Del Sarto's fine excuse:
"Some good son
Paint my two hundred pictures –
Let him try."
And rationalised it thus:
Doubled in involvement,
Caught in each other's wish
Or love,
Or weakness,
Or what was,
In all emergent masochisms on earth,
Lamed by each other's glance
Our sort walk silent in a false compassion

Past acres of the darkening summer sea.
The rich have all the luxury of quarrel
And the offended stance.

Anterior silence mars
Even these broken thoughts.

Reticent father who
Exampled me in some
Virtues I could not reach
With which I now dispense
Or even must attack,
I see you in your world
From where I walk in mine
Through the same childish eye:
Your racket and your twine,
Your Parkers red and black,
The Standard Little Nine,
The smell of creosote
Of wood and paraffin,
The bay's blue undulance,
Swelling horizon line,
Your nicotine stained hand,
The hut at Ardamine,
Obsessional offerings to
Some sort of order ... what
Did you hope to gain?

The pattern of your life intrigued my thought,
Strange pattern with its curious return
To die across spring-tossed Drumcondra Road
By chance from where by chance you had been born,
A Dubliner. And yet the obscure powers
Work patterns, bring returns, conjunctions,
Even from what looks like chance or drift.

I take this too, along with all the rest,
A late inheritance, another parting gift.

ON COMPILING ENTRIES FOR AN ENCYCLOPEDIA

For Norman Stewart

All the sad clichés of the old editions:
"An early disappointment of the heart",
"Habitually despairing cast of mind",
"His hopes of public favour dashed again",
"Long hours of arduous and ill-paid toil",
"Constant recourse to alcohol and drugs",
"A constitution weakened by excess",
Spring up with wry renewable effect
As I hack out biographies tonight.
Romantic, minor, victims of their *zeitgeist*,
Cloaked in their common repertory despairs,
They coughed and caught their final colds and died.
"An early disappointment of the heart".
We all might smile. But there is nothing comic
In Clarence Mangan's misery or mask.
And Dowson haunts the histories of fame.
Stab every cliché with an irony
Previous compilers did not know was needed
They're true enough of some, perhaps of most.
I between jigs and reels had colleagues also,
Mocked mockers, drunk with trouble, to whom now
I see such cliché dooms could well apply.
Does then the mere vocation in itself
Unfit some men for life? Or men unfitted
Turn to the childish refuge of the word?
Or is it that the practice of this art
Is guilt avoiding self-indulgence for
Those whom the "public favour" may elude
And accident refuses to prop up
So that they stumble to an early grave
Under a compound burden: explanation
To make which is itself another crime?
Well turn the page again. An aged one,
Who held on past irrelevance and loss,
Smooths his grey hairs and leans upon a hand
Which opened lock and casket. He is fierce.
For all their lost authority is his.

FAMILIAR

"I only knew one poet in my life
And this, or something like it, was his way,"
Begins the Browning poem, and we all
Have in our contrite hearts a notion which
Recollected still may still reveal
Something about the poetry we seek.

The poet is the poetry of course.

When this familiar tutelary walks
Over the bridge to Searson's for a pint
Or further on to Mirrelson's for a bet
On a bright morning in the month of May,
His conscience satisfied and some loose cash,
Water and weeds, Palladian Portobello,
A second-hand sewing machine in Christy Bird's,
The muttering old mad wan and the mini
Skirted lovely stork legged unattemptress,
The westward stretch of sky towards Harold's Cross
Are local harmonies to his localled heart.
Not all he sees is faultless, and it's even
Hard to cross the Canal Road for the traffic:
But no nonentity now feeds his fear
Of failure or oblivion or disturbs
The giant love he feels for all the show,
From Kelly's Corner to his moving shoes.
He has no job, except the one he does,
And for himself, he, providence, provides.
No Fine Gael ambitions itch his hand.
The poem, well begun, will soon be finished.
Its marvels daze the reader in his mind
At intervals while he salutes himself
Or talks at length with Tom behind the bar.
Because he walks, upsides with all the world:

Not that he has, but that he is, such friends.

ANOTHER VERSION

In another version* of the story, Deirdre,
Bound, is given over to the King and is
"A year in Conor's couch".
He must have had great sport with that sad captive,
Lambent expanses stretched beneath his hand,
Small belly, breasts and throat, lean thighs pulled wide,
And all the beauty of her back and hummocks.
She may have even writhed in response
While she lay hating him, ferocious eyes
Burning beneath tossed hair.
Did he possess much?
Or a little only?
More than most dream?
Or less than the poorest lovers?
The story says he tried to soothe her, did he then
Sometimes pathetically wheedle and cajole?
The more fool he.
Perhaps he came each night, a hang-dog lover,
And fucked her in the dark when he was spurned
Quickly and shamefully while all that wealth
Lay spread beneath him for the somehow taking.

A year she spent. With Conor every night.
The story says she never smiled. No wonder.
Ate and slept little, stayed there every day
In that soiled couch, her head upon her knees,
Named her dead Naoise when he spoke to her.

At length he asked her what most stoked her hate.
"Yourself and Owen, son of Duthrecht," said she.
"Very well," Conor said, a man of spirit,
King and the son of Kings, and maybe tiring
Of this unequal contest,
"You'll spend a year in Owen's couch," and had her
Taken, still bound, to him who'd killed her lover.
She spent that night stretched out for Owen's pleasure,
Who was no lover, no old maudlin softy,
Nor no High King whose wish was to unburden,
Heart to heart talking, all the cares of office.

*The oldest, in "The Book of Leinster" (transcribed c. 1150 AD). In the others
Deirdre throws herself into the open grave in which her lover Naoise is being
buried and dies there.

Next day at Muirthemne there was assemblage,
Nobles and people, lawyers, poets, pedants,
The tale well-known to all and this new twisting,
And what did the bold Owen do but had her
Brought in his chariot, his prize, behind him,
So that all saw what he had now for plaything.
Conor drove up.
She looked down at the ground, the story says,
So that she might not see her gallants smiling.
Did Conor smile?
Putting a brave face on it?
Man to man?
Conspirator in relish?
Laugh?
With Owen?
"Well, Deirdre," said he, boldly boasting, "it's
The look a ewe gives between rams, the glance
You cast between myself and Owen now."
There was a high rock there.
She hurled herself,
Head stretched to strike it, from the chariot.
When they held
The thin-ribbed body each had held before
It had less will and less response than ever.
The story ends there, doesn't tell if Conor
Gazed on the dead girl, what he felt and thought
He'd lost, if anything, or any more.

THE MAN WHO WENT ABSENT FROM THE NATIVE LITERATURE

He did not come of a long line of stone cutters,
Wise but silent men who had learned silence from the stone,
Or seamen, whose eyes reflected distance,
Though there isn't much distance in the alleyways and man-
    cupboards of a modern ship;
His lot were not even Dubliners with the desperate generosity
    of the Dublin slums,
Expressed through drink in the grimy man-traps where the
    generosity of working class men found its profitable-to-
    others outlet,
Nor were they doctors whose hands had calmed heartbeats
    and children in the womb
As well as dealing cards nightly in the bridge club,
Or savants, careless of advancement and intent only on
    learning,
Unlike any savants you might have the misfortune to meet
    today.
And they were certainly not aristocrats whose blood had
    darkened the dim banners in the village church like wine-
    stains
And ran in the veins of the village children as proof of
    everybody's careless virility.

His mother was not the sort who put other people, but
    especially sentimental men, in mind of the Great Earth
    Goddess, Everybody's Mother.
She was a neurotic woman, much given to dyspepsia and
    novenas, especially the Nine Fridays,
And so far from being careless and bountiful and all-
    embracing like nature,
Spewing out children and other creations like a volcano
    giving out rocks,
When he know her anyway she emanated mostly anxiety,
And the only things she seemed to want to take in were
    money, priests' opinions and stories about girls who were in
    trouble.
Nor were his grandmas, so far as he knew, any more outgoing
    or disdainful of consequence.
At the times he met them he never heard anything but words
    of caution about knocking over ornaments and not getting

wet on the way to school from them,
Expressed in stale musty clichés in musty stale parlours,
Where, in any case any ideas about saving the world might
    have been generated over the odd drop of sherry,
Several representations of a mauled, battered, eviscerated and
    totally dispirited saviour and his broken-hearted mother
    were exhibited to dispel them,
Even Parnell, even Robert Emmet being absent from those
    walls.

You couldn't say either that such and such a landscape had
    helped to mould him or his ancestors.
His forebears were not gaunt upland people, slow of speech
    but unshakable once decided,
Some of them might have been of course, but the reasons for
    the slowness of speech if any in the more proximate cases of
    his da and ma
Were the obvious dangers of small-town life;
And his daddy as a matter of fact kept decisions to a
    minimum and was easily dissuaded from anything except a
    drink.
Nor were they mountainy men whose feuds and lovings
    became legends in the peaceful valleys.
Any family scandal he sniffed in the wind was of a different
    order.
Nor yet, not to make a meal of it, secretive canny folk from
    the back of the hill.
They were secretive all right, and canny in their way, but
    there was no known hill that had anything to do with them.

And he came in any case from what you might call mixed and
    migrant stock,
Who in the era of petty officialdom and jobs for the more
    educated
Had been stationed here, transferred there, married
    somewhere else,
And so the town he was born in was an accident for his
    parents,
And a much more serious, nearly fatal, to the spirit anyway,
    one for him.
When he thought of it afterwards he did not think of colourful
    characters,
Ne'er-do-wells with a turn of phrase, charming rapscallions

with a gleam in their eyes and the arse nearly out of their
  breeches,
Idling down by the river where the chestnut trees cast their
  nets,
Friends of his father or otherwise.
As a matter of fact his father had no friends.
He did not see it all as picturesque.
Wherever the picturesque was it was not there.
And the local colour the place had was the colour of shame,
For him anyway,
His memories memories of idiotic burgeonings and incoherent
  mistakes,
The mistakes of an ignorant outsider with the wrong
  enthusiasms
Whose first loves were based on false premises.

And so, granted that in his heart there was a sort of void,
Unfilled by images of the Greyhound Racing Track, the
  Arcadia Dance Hall and the Cattle Dealers' Cathedral of his
  native place,
Or the memory of companions who had sometimes diverted
  him,
While he undoubtedly diverted them,
That the tendrils that would root had found no soil
Comparable to the rich ploughlands and pastures of pastoral
  epic
In the asphalt of the school playground or the ashy soil of the
  backyard,
And you could say that he was a man without a tribe,
Pariah wandering on the outskirts, by woods and streams not
  his;
And though for years he felt that these lackings of stone-cutter
  ancestors and comic, picturesque characters among his
  father's friends
Made him somehow inferior in blood and in bone to those
  who had them
Or said they had,
Nevertheless:
He did not bang a local drum.
He did not give a hoot who won the tribal conflicts.
He didn't want anybody to win.
Nor did he think that your ancestors' creations, folk-songs

and folk-lore,
Or come-all-ye's and war-cries,
Made you somehow creative yourself if you made enough
    fuss about them
And got money from the radio by doing it.
Neither did he flog a line in identity whether real or false,
Nor in the picturesque,
Whatever that is,
He did not think that the local hero was more real than the
    unlocal one.
When he walked through cities he was not always yearning
    for the soft pints and softer options of the pubs where his
    playmates drank.
He thought that *du sang, de la volupté et de la mort*
He would learn as much on his travels as in his native
    province.
He did not think that the cabin where the rain came in under
    the door was free from sordidity;
And thought in any case that the sordid we had always with
    us;
But that when it came to the sordid
Metropolitan sordidity was richer and more fecund.
And that when it came to freedom,
Which it would come to in the end,
The metropolis if it was a real metropolis would have
    freedoms which would astonish any peasant who ever lived,
Or any picturesque character from our world of misfortune
    either.
And that when there were free men on this earth
They would strike a balance with their ancestors
Which would not begin in regret,
Or in nostalgia,
Or in lies.

HOMAGE TO THE RURAL WRITERS, PAST AND PRESENT, AT HOME AND ABROAD

Country origins, country roots
Seduce long after our transplantment,
The mechanic round, the mud-caked boots
Retain or gain a strange enchantment.

The endurance of the rural breed
Seems, like the rugged landscape, stoical.
Rural grasping, rural greed,
Are somehow, unlike ours, heroical.

The rural rancour, dampened down,
The rural passions, smouldering, steaming,
The rural smile, the rural frown,
Compared to ours are realer seeming.

And when two rural lovers meet,
Escaping rural interdiction,
The rural suddenness and heat,
Intemperate, beyond restriction,

Which visits all with complex dooms,
With family feuds and endless fighting
Has still involved the primal grooms
In passionate, envied, early plighting.

While haze on the long barrow's back,
The winter-misted lane's sad squelchings,
Great nature's oozings and her wrack,
Unlike our factory chimney's belching,

Endorse their ardours as intense,
Not like our own, which are verbal, flagging,
Ensure they show no grain of sense,
Remove the reasonable and the nagging;

Till kindly nature takes away
The rougher, rawer edge of feeling,
Shows them the main-spring of the play,
The moral tragedy revealing,

And country habitudes, country ways
Reconcile all to nature's purpose.
The floorboards creak, the house decays
And no surprise will now disturb us.

The realer seeming spade has struck,
The realer seeming sod is turning.
All lie in realer seeming muck,
While autumn leaves are really burning.

FOR THE DAMNED PART

There was never any acquaintance
That was not in some way marred,
Remembrance or later meeting
But something in it jarred:
Nothing altogether tellable,
Nothing fully redeemed,
Needing no emendation,
Being actually what it seemed.
There was usually something over.
There was almost always deceit.
No door was ever closed on
The exorcised or complete.

This is the way the world goes,
The dead twig in the ground,
The bottle by the lakeside
While winter gathers round.
Creatures of both we hide in
Dimensions of time and space.
Let the immortal spirits look
Each other in the face.

A FORM OF ELEGY FOR THE POET BRIAN HIGGINS (1930–1965)

These strange cessations ...
Brian Higgins who
Scurried like tree-mouse hunched from here to there,
Eyes live with doubt and worry about loonch:
Crouched in the corners of his muckers' kitchens,
Frantic with answers, poems, begging letters:
Who hoped to doss all time away, and did;
Though he'd Hesperian summers in his heart
And knew as much as most of the good life:
Is now not even "beyond" our praise and carping,
For he was always that, but rather is
Utterly ended, but for memories,
Misinformation, poems, principles,
Or, speaking of the latter, lack of them,
None of which now have aught to do with 'im.

How does one write an elegy for zero?
Address a nothingness, "Dear friend, etcet"?
Exhort the audience, "Give 'im the bays"?
Ambiguously or otherwise proclaim
We shall not live to look upon his like?
We shall a bit. He was like life all right.
And life much more like him than most admit.
For reasons he was accurate about.
Which is the poet's function. One might twine
Him in somehow with what he never now
Will see again, the trees, the roots, the wall,
And dragging Arnold's nature to his aid
Perpetuate the pantheistic flux.
The truth is that he didn't look at much.
Or since in part at least he was a poet
In order to escape (like any pug)
Perhaps it's right to list the things he's missing:
Either green furniture and servitude,
Or turning friendships into trading posts:
The wearing misconceptions of his claim
Simple refusal to participate
(Apart, let's keep it clean, from his vocation)
Provoked among the watchers at the bar

Who with each watch bewailed his dear time's waste –
"You're not quite eminent enough for that.
More famous poets have ordinary jobs".
And he, except there is no him, escapes
Self torture through each day's comparison
Of real individuality's
Gummed, dusty budding with the all around
Slick summer other sorts of plants enjoy:
The contrast of his littered corner with
Tidy interiors of inferior lives,
And stung by every liar the conscious, comic
Knowledge that most are hunchbacks in the dark,
That Coeur de Lion, Papa Hem and Lawrence,
Ludmilla Tcherneyava, Marie Stopes,
Suburban hard-chaws and rich layabouts
Were none as couth as most of them made out.

And yet all this won't do, he had his laughs
And even loves, his muckers and his mocks,
His mornings in the hay, washed socks and chats,
Poems and paradoxes, fish and chips,
His visions and affections and himself.
He's missing these and we are missing much
Of which it might be possible to write
Now this odd individual avatar
Of much the world won't have as truth is dead.
But he's the one who's missing the whole lot,
The mathematics of all gain and loss,
The texture of the morning and the day,
And such the nullity and wastage there
I must adopt the fiction of my kind,
The human fiction and address my friend
And lapsing into fallacy just say,
You should be with us, here is company.

REDUCTIONIST POEM
(1981)

for Paul Durcan

Youth, not age, is our time of renunciation,
Of retreat into memory and dream:
The shaft of dusty sunlight through the barred window of the
  basement room,
The bare white plastered wall with the single emblem,
The long self-communings under the torn October trees.
And those destroyed by the forms just barely disclosed,
The haunting perfections that Plato saw beyond,
Are not easy to persuade into contingency.
He who has once seen it, says Plotinus,
Laughs at all other loves and despises what he thought
  beautiful before.
Loving with a loyal passion and a piercing longing
He does not appreciate as he did the litheness of other bodies.
The one profile, the one lost gaze consumes their growing
  time
As the autumn flames consume the leaves.

And in despair of what is called order,
Perhaps of existence itself,
There are those who have dreamed of imposing a new
  geometry
On the haphazard conjunctions of the office blocks,
The glass of the encased men shattered by the bomb-blast,
Descending in cleansing sheets to the empty pavements,
The buying and selling stopped and the constant
  diminishments.
Yet the gratitude of the nations has been theirs as well,
Black and red banners flapping against great Corinthian
  columns,
The happy faces in the huge square a carpet for the dream.
For the heart cannot rest among the ill considered spaces of
  the raw suburbs
Where the spring wind twitches the new bushes
And the fearful but ambitious families live, each behind its
  fence,
Nor among the high-rise towers which have size without
  permanence
And are homes without reassurance.
There are only a few squares and a few fountains.
There are only a few man-made places where the heart can be
  at rest,

Where the entablature rests on the columns as they on the
   steps.
He who has once seen it says Plotinus
Remembers with a supreme passion and an unpacifiable
   longing.
Disgust and rage are their portion,
Greater even than the old slobberer's disgust and rage.

But the Platonists speak now too with amber and velvet
   voices
And induce a dream in the many who can be statistically
   numbered.
The lives of the murmuring dark and the shadow-lives were
   once separate.
In the torchlight the usherette's hands could be seen and the
   ends of her frayed white trousers.
But the screen has expanded outwards now like a fine
   translucent gum bubble.
It has bulged through the living rooms and encompassed the
   lives of the houses.
All are within its cocoon
And the stubborn projections dissolve to
Perspective without abutment,
Collision without shock,
Surface without texture,
The unfitting detail removed
From the landscape as from the event,
The gristle and shit from the violence.
Even from tragedy,
Even from the unhappiness of children,
The true, the awful drag
The waiting and fear are removed.
It is never raining as you wait
At the Metropole cinema
Watching the traffic lights change.
The last bus has not gone.
The blow has not fallen.
Somebody is alive.
There is more than loneliness.
There is explainable circumstance.
No one is now isolated
In a unique dilemma.

Everyone exists in a recognised,
Accountable plot situation
Or a sociological category,
Even the suicides.

Like an aphid she taps the screen for the milk of the dream.
He takes a room in Sachs. He knows how to make these
    arrangements.
Of course you need a few quid, but if you're in the know it's
    easy.
I'd like to buy the world a Coke and keep it company.
Blue Stratos. Get it on. Feel young. Feel free.
Now Bioterm makes everybody more beautiful.
Maybelline stays on all day stays on all night and
    conditions your lashes every minute you wear it.
The Bunny is a global symbol.
Christmas is aftershave.
Happiness is a good cigar.
The legend in your lifetime: Mercedes-Benz.

And from manipulated America, land
Of the enormous dream
In the peasant's bent shoulders,
Come at last
The TV families
Whose hair can be lifted,
Pushed back, hangs and flops,
Is not fuzzy or wiry
And whose denimed behinds are little and cute,
The girls all tom-boys and the boys all ultimately manly and
    kind,
The adolescent traumas only such as maw and paw can find
    out about,
Patterned little worries that they can tearfully smile over
In their own retreat, the bedroom.
As she begins to unbutton they remember
Their date for the graduation dance,
Not so long ago, well, say twenty years,
Before marriage and maturity chimed in.
He smilingly takes her,
Still a little shy, in his arms and
Unbuttons for her.

The scene dissolves. Naturally.
Middle-aged sex does nothing for the viewer.
But what a model Maw is.
Especially in slacks.
And what a model Paw.
With his pipe and his carpentry.
This is better than the Irish Catholic family,
That simulacrum of the Holy Family,
Any day of the week.
The Holy Family had no sex between Maw and Paw,
No adolescents, no automobiles,
But this way the problems are subsumed and vanish.
The boys can all use the car and learn chivalry early.
We can all approve the patterns of the peer group date.
She used to read the Confessions magazines as a corrective.
The real underground literature she said they were.
The things I did to satisfy boys. I was the neighbourhood
    service station.
You can never keep a boy like him to yourself: still,
Girls like me will do anything to try.
The special sex dreams fat girls have.

At sixteen how eager we were for the union of Souls:
Bodies, except she was so beautiful it made a union of some
    sort
Seem the only thing that mattered,
Perhaps a bit of a drawback.
And not much detail, in memory anyway, although
The sensation of the nipple when first touched
Unforgettable, not even the eyes' colour now,
Nor qualities of the mind either, or temperament, since.
Truth to tell, little enough was known
About any of these things except her crooked smile
And way of saying "golly".
She displaced specifics, "blinding
The beholder with beauty". She almost displaced the world.
And what one wanted was some sort of a declaration.
A declaration perhaps progressing by stages,
The hand lingering on the shoulder for a while longer.
After getting down off the wall during the walk along the
    Abbey path,
The hand touched and taken in the scented darkness of the

Astor cinema,
The hand round the back of the neck:
Parts of the declaration,
The shy statement of a returned wish for everlasting
    togetherness,
And an end to all disunion, imperfection, separation.
For the girl the full fuck only a pledge of togetherness
    anyway,
Part of the dear dream, and, hopefully at least, a way of
    entering into a bond.

And the dream of cohesion is the commonest dream.
Boy and girl together against the world.
Boy sacrificing himself for comrades and comradeship.
The young savant thinking:
My name will be known with the others.

To cease to be
A mere imperfect part of a Lost Whole
Crying out for return and re-union,
Finding here no fit abode and longing,
With how acute a longing
To come home to the Heart of Things,
The Centre,
Without Divergence or Discordance,
At last, and
Forever and ever, Amen.

And in this everyday existence
Where sometimes we glimpse only,
A girl on a moving staircase,
Hair and skirt blowing backward,
What we thirst for ever after,
Or do not even glimpse,
Seeing with greater intensity in the imagination,
Yes, we are tortured by dreams.

The two hollow hemispheres of the human cerebellum are so
    large
That to fit within the heavy plates of the skull
They have become deeply folded and convoluted.
This enormity of the frontal and temporal lobes

Is particularly characteristic of man,
As is the fact that they include
Among their millions of nerve cells
Myriads not enslaved to exact functions
But given over merely to the storing of memories and their
    association.
Man is an image-making animal.
And also man is equipped with a specially sensitive spot on
    the retina of the eye
Which accounts for his greater acuteness of vision.
And what he sees he can remember.
He can, as we say, imagine.
And what he has never seen he can synthesise from what he
    has.
He mixes memory and desire.
He can, as we say, imagine.
And sorrow's crown of sorrows is remembering happier
    things.
Or imagining them.

We are the image-makers,
We are the dreamers of dreams,
World losers and world forsakers,
Envisaging bluer sea-breakers
And much less desolate streams.

But as Robert Browning said
"Never the time and the place
And the loved one all together,"
Never the precise circumstance
That we would if we could construct.

In the cool noon-tide place by the lake shore,
Beneath the trees,
Where on the leaf-shadowed café table's green and white
    chequered cloth
The blue soup bowl, bread and wine are set,
We talk with our true friends,
Familiar but breath-taking still in thought and look,
Whose charm and beauty,
Dark lashes resting an instant and in the breeze a blonde
    strand straying,

Or whose notorious adventures
Are neither an insult nor a deprivation.
Who have never betrayed us
And with whom we have never wished a word unsaid or an
  act undone.
Like the heat welling up through the coolness in the dusk
  hour
The emotions of one intermingle with those of another;
And after the definitions which appease
The ravening desire for clarity and explanation,
But as we know can sometimes rend,
The complete comradeship still reigns.

The men are for intellectual companionship
And comradeship in the struggle,
The women for falling in love with,
For reflecting the rich depth of the day
And the dazzlement of the talk,
Of the life we lead
And of ourselves.

"On what poor stuff our manhood's dreams were fed"
Till we too "learned what dole of vanity
Would serve a human soul for daily bread."
And the friend I have is not the perfect friend.
The poem I write is not the perfect poem.
Any more than this tiny bedroom with its book and paper
  strewn bed
And the wallpaper I did not choose
Is the perfect room.
The children playing relievio, the ball
Bouncing off the back wall, disturb, distract.
The hard shadows of spring grow shorter at the gable ends
As the days grow longer.
The harmony we experience is not shaped
Or free from all but planned discordance
Like a certain kind of art.
Even in the hour when Hesperus is mirrored in the still water
When the veins of the body suffuse with tenderness
As the sky with the mauve and violet tones of evening
And your companion's touch and gesture are continuing
  evidence

Of that gratification which William Blake thought
The one we most rejoice to believe another has experienced,
We again become conscious
Not only of other human activity,
A drunk arguing at the street corner,
A train hooting at the crossing,
The power station sighing in the dusk,
But of our separate existences one from another
With our egocentric concerns.
And even the moment of most complete release
Is not untinged by fore and afterthought,
Regret and comparison.
Perhaps the thought of a greater plenitude missed,
Even the very ecstasy is haunted by an absence.

But nevertheless an abundant reality
In the shock of another's being,
The dark, hair-shadowed mound,
The body, rich in blemish, moved by tides;
In the skin, returning licence to the shaded light,
In the rich undulance of the flesh,
And its answering intumescences;
As in the afterwards gentle touch,
The contours of the happy face,
In the beauty which is now a friend
And no longer a taunt or a severance
An almost total and
A hypostatic joy.

But to affirm is now the most difficult thing of all.
We can still be funny
About the sad mistake or the lost opportunity,
Cruel about the phoniness and the error, knowing
The salt smart will preserve the words from corruption.
But in the age of the advertising managers and the image
    makers,
The manhood asserters of the bed and bull-ring,
Whose narcissism is so strong they must continually prove
    their response
To an outer reality
We have learned to distrust the words which describe life's
    richness.

And fearing inflation of language more than its shrivelling
What shall we say when the summer holds and brings us
The gaze without guile and the simple answering gesture
The skirt turning with the body and the brown hair turning
    with the head
In the unfeigned delight of the first greeting?

We have words for the smart and salt of the wound but the
    salt of the clear
Skin and the salt of the bread and butter,
The dusk of the day when the work was accomplished,
When our friends were open and the links were strong,
When summer lulled the Kensington avenues
And the painters returned
With their arms full of food and wine
And the conversation was joyful and serious
With a sense of work accomplished,
Work to be done,
The great makers honoured,
While the plane trees hung their branches down
From which leaves issued like folios
Are almost impossible to celebrate today.

And so will not abandon either
A rational human hope
That all might live
In harmony with proper human purpose,
Buoyant on the city's neon waves,
The complete man touching others always
And being touched by them
Being utterly dependent
On love or fellowship,
Never free from this dependence,
Even on the long days
With a book in the hot roof-well,
Or the self-sufficing hours
Watching the logs burn
While the stag roared in the wood.

As the traffic heaves and surges
North along Hampstead Road
Every fifth car a Rolls

A part of him fiercely longs
Not only for love and money
Becoming in any case synonymous
And a place at least equal in dignity
To that of a B.B.C. producer
Or a visiting Irish one
But for his words to be a part
Of an all-in performance
At the Unity Theatre in August
Red Star over the proscenium
Requiring sets by Colquhoun
And a cast not only of bus-men
But of girl dancers as well
And statement not abandoned
Or the precise word despised
Girl acrobats with supple backs
With whom he might fall in love.

For gone are the days of the wired single-engined monoplane
Clinging to height,
Valves sucking the night air,
And propeller churning the fog.
Spanners and maps in the glove pocket,
The spatter of misfiring,
As the trembling wings describe
Their over-deliberate arc.
One man reading green dials
And then after black night with
Sparks flying from the cylinder cluster
Peering ahead for land
Coming in over rock-thin foamline
And the blotchy whitewashed cabins
Of a green island with blue
Even for Irish bachelors
Squinting from the half door
Which the rain had come in under
Spluttering a new hope.

And the one alone home-coming hero would of course meet
    his match,
The bare shouldered radiant blonde,
Delicate and defenceless as a Dresden figurine.

Look into the china-blue eyes, though.
There is not much sign of an answering soul.
And regard that calm expression,
Not much troubled by brain either.
Nor, in spite of the wide-eyed, worshipping,
Even anticipatory gaze,
Is there much evidence that she understands
The home-coming hero's needs.
For really, compared to what
Might be thought to be the case with others,
With Brigid, for example, dark-haired, frowning, brooding,
Or Philomena, a bit on the fat side but all go and sloppy give,
This self-contained and willow-pliant one,
A hand-span across the small of the straight back,
Every curl and strap in place,
Does not really seem to promise much
In the way of sexual responses,
Or, say, failing responses,
What he would in the end, alas,
Settle for, concessions.
In fact since the general impression is even of a sort of sex excluding
Blonde fastidiousness as a way of life,
A philosophy of the sheathed bloom,
We have a bit of a mystery here.
What is the potent attraction which so maddens the home–coming hero?
Is it even the fragility itself,
The radiance that could be disarrayed,
The helplessness so great or to be perilous for its possessor
Which account for this welling up of power within him,
This desire to hold safe and enfold?

Someone so appealing,
An enormous appeal in the enlarged china-blue eyes,
So obviously in need of a male arm,
So sweetly defenceless,
Can of course be dominated
By the male protector.
So could the dream then even be
To get this radiant perfect being
Down into the hot arena where all are one,

To show her what makes the hero,
What defencelessness really means,
Who's master around here,
And by dealing so with this perfection
To increase, however metaphysically difficult that may be,
By a process of subjugation and osmosis,
The degree of his male own?

And the hero too in the battle
For the old lost cause again,
The hope that called to boyhood,
The flag once again on the walls,
The mountaineers stubborn and steadfast
As the guns boom in the passes
While the trim girls wait for the wounded,
Worshippers of the brave,
The braid looped from each shoulder,
Gloves at the peaked caps' brim,
The bellies slightly bulging
Under the Sam Browne belts,
The king in the dark glasses trembling
After a night in the chalet
With the teen-age English dancer
Who gets two hundred a week
For swallowing his sperm.

On the road between the olive trees
The men behind the ox-carts
And the men on the mules returning,
Still hungry at nightfall,
In the clear dusk of the south
While the women complain at the well,
A child clutching a skirt
With an unhealed scab on its lip
Are not community either
Whatever Roland sung.
In the city's hazy sunlight
Where the dockers desisting from dominoes
Spit when the bones of the little boy saint
Pass under their canopy,
The candle in the governor's hand
Its thin flame pleading.

They have seen the money power
Taking hold of the streets.
The ambassador poet may mourn
For the Prince D'Aquitaine
At the Tour Abolie
But the real Prince sits on the board
Of the Chase Manhattan Bank,
Despite his Sèvres collection
His pleasures the realised dreams
Of the average sensual male,
His grasp of business admired,
The screams from the barracks unheard
In the cool of the summer night.

And the archbishop with turkey jowls
Believes also in hierarchical order
As instance of heavenwards here.
In return for resignation
All will get their reward:
A peace as deep blue as the eastern sky at angelus,
A coolness as in the flagged transept,
A beauty softer and bluer than that of the banked flowers,
A rest longer even than on Sunday
When the satiated man sleeps
Beside his aching wife,
Even the little ones sleep
And the mother of twelve is herself a child
Coming home in tears to comfort,
To the wisdom of heavenly parents,
Skirt clutch and hand hold
And an end to all contradiction
And the awful burdens of love.

As even the philosophers yearn
For an end to the complexities and contradictions
Which challenge unendingly the intellect and moral sense of
    man
But do not overbear it,
Necessity competing with necessity,
Justice competing with justice,
Consideration with consideration,
Time and resource

Precluding time and resource.
And though at every ascent that we can know
As individuals or as a species
The complexities and contradictions become more acute
It is through seeking resolution
Of each apparent contradiction
That man moves towards life
And not through abandonment
Or the dream of peace.

Why don't we all pull together like during the war?
In Flanders we was all pals.

And in full masculine chorus
The marching boys sing out,
The banners like sails on masts
The Platonic ranks drawn up.
The men on the saluting base
As the booted columns pass,
Young lads faces fresh
With the bloom of stupidity
And the gleam of hope
Have murdered the dialecticians
Who insisted on contradiction
Have murdered the complex loves
Of the poets at large in the morning
By the fire in the glass-bright pub,
Have murdered the poets themselves
And the possibilities inherent
In the allocation of resource
For the human purposes mingling
Like the lovers in the park,
The barriers broken between them,

Between action and contemplation
Between one life and the other
And between the sexes a comradeship
An ease like a boy's ease
Never known in the old world.

Just as the priest, who, with a dramatic gesture throwing back
The cape of his soutane and raising blunt fingered hands
To the virgin towards whom all the candle flames aspire,

Embowered among blue hydrangeas on the altar,
Murdered the gentle blooming
Of sex even in dreams.

It is where the false order is imposed,
The queue shuffling past with spoon and plate
And on the tiles of the lavatory walls excrement is daubed,
That the sordidness wells back
In the cold morning
And becomes the governing principle
Of our life thereafter.

Down the concrete staircase a small soft tornado blows the
    litter
And blows it swirling back up.
On the landings the wire grilles have been bent, the bulbs
    broken or stolen.
On the fourth floor an old lady crouches every night before
    the meaningless television.
She is terrified of the dark stairs.
On the eighth a young mother with pale skin puffed like
    rising dough
Waits for the moment when the small hot point finally
    vanishes
And she stares at the sudden dirty opacity of the screen.
She knows he will come home drunk on the labour money
    tonight
And climb on her in the dark without a word
Shagging and grunting for half an hour or more
His prick slipping out more than once
The sour beer smell on his breath.
Today she was afraid that the little one might fall.
Then that she might throw herself.
The soft tornadoes that enter the stairway disturb
The accuracy of the planners' dream.
In the entry where the unbreakable bulbs have been broken
Casual hate has its moment,
And sometimes casual love,
Having written its messages on the walls,
Can breathe them into another.

But however great the contradiction
Between the collective and freedom

Under the hydraulically pre-stressed
White soaring ferroconcrete roof-planes
The switches ensure dependence.
Though the spanners gone from the glove pocket,
The workers go from the floor
Not to what makes sense to a child
Or a young girl fiercely dreaming
Between the sand dunes,
Under the railway bridge,
But to what can be explained only
In terms of our exhaustion and inertia.
Who have whispered in the front parlour under the crown of
    thorns,
Who have watched the endless football on the big set in the
    boozer,
Who have brought the protesting children to the old people's
    home every Sunday
And sat at the formica tables singing, "I did it my way".

And not for the money God
Who is worshipped by clammy men
Dying in the blue lit sauna
And by the wombless bridge players,
Cheeks purple under grey powder
And feared in the semi-detached
Three bedroom dream home
Where the oblong moon
Devours the children
While the children look on
To be thrown
Like a terrier into a terrier pit
Into competition with one's fellows
And refuse also a number
In the big room with the desks
Where all are encased in glass,
The accelerator's splurge
The last splurge of the soul,
The procreation, the pension
Justifying a life,
The children the extended antennae
Of middle-aged ego advancement,
Pushed out cautiously

Feeling the unknown
In search of further possession
Retracted immediately
When it proves to be alive.

For our days are caricatures
Of the days we might have
As the children know, hearing the door bang
And the voices raised in quarrel; as the couple know
Dreaming under the willows and aspen their mutual dream,
The tenderness of bodies flowing like a river
Through the summer days;
The boy making a scale model of the old Bristol;
The poet measuring wastage like an engineer;
As the girl knows coming home at six o'clock
To another friendless evening in the plywood partitioned
    room;
The playwright, waking in the morning, the solution like a
    revelation,
Glad to be himself and to live in a world of such problems;
As all know, who pine in repetition and drudgery
For tasks which absorb, suggest and re-vivify.

We are bred to a gradual acceptance,
To a forfeiture of dream,
Repeating our parents' errors,
Aching for the sudden shock of the blow and the salt sting,
Mistaking acceptance for courage,
Bringing the best part of our nature to bear on the pointless
    endurance,
Making sacrifices for those who really want something else.
And the merchants of fear and despair present themselves
    always
On the high altars erected in the stadia
As the prophets of selfless love.

Though in this pay your way existence haunted by dreams
Where time is remorseless in its foreclosures
And the moment of consummation is the moment of
    dissatisfaction;
Where we never, still less in art, achieve perfection,
Where conflicting claims may have to remain in conflict,

The time for one thing against the time for another,
The resource for one thing against the resource for another,
The love for one thing against the love for another;
And though not always as now when resource is money and
love possession,
Perhaps always
The pity for one against the love of another,
We must learn to rejoice in the fact that
Everything intermingles
And everything conflicts,
That a lesser thing can be a joy
And a substitute a delight.

Stress and division create. The tensile strength makes the span
possible.
Frozen music perhaps, but music with mass and dependence.
The planes of the roofs intersect. The gables' abutments are
haphazard.
In abutments and intersections a strange deep sense
satisfaction.
Place your hand on the wall. Touch brick. Feel the mortar
crumble.
The groove and the scar are our being. We gouge out the
earth to make home of it.
Made safe, made fast, in shelter, with friends, food, fire and
light.
In the wanting before, in the lucky to have is the greater
delight and plenitude,
The shutter just hasped, the storm shut out, the quarrel
forgotten, the love flow,
As in a furnished room
With the saucepan on the gas ring
And the bus fare for tomorrow
Though only the books from the library
And the landlord across the hall
Between two trusting people
A satisfaction of sense
A bright circle of time
A little republic of love.

NOT EASY

"'Fool,' said my Muse to me,
'Look in thy heart and write',"
A still delight-giving member of the poetic fraternity,
The noble Philip Sidney
Averred. And though some have accounted it good advice.

It is not in fact that easy
To see inside such a complicated, mazily wired
Piece of machinery:
Wired for deceit you might say.
And in any case not everybody is prepared to so look and
    accordingly write.

There are some who are simply too cowardly.
Some take a peek and decide
What's in there is not for them, then turn to the tulip and
    proceed to number it's streaks.
Some bow, in fear or otherwise, to the claims of ideology.
And some even today would suffer trepidation at the thought
    of the result being read by the lady wife.

While to complicate matters further, if we deal in duties
It may be that the outer world needs our strict pens to see it
    and to set it right.
One can have a little too much poking around inside a la
    Bloomsbury.
The great mileage machines are religion or ideology.
And, yes, one can love and not want to dismay someone who
    has perhaps tacitly or otherwise accepted a description of
    one's heart or it's workings that was slightly simplified.

Of course, this last can be avoided to some extent and one
    might also be enabled to describe more coolly
What goes on in the organ concerned by pretending that the
    owner of same is not the shuffling old I.
Avoiding clog, degrees of shame, wrong tone of voice,
    appearance of self-pity:
All these may sometimes be accomplished by what is
    nowadays called the adoption of personae,
Though the next thing you find is that the personae are

neither you nor personae, but interesting, exciting or
charming, fellows, and probably with lives which are more
believable than your own and thus more easily described.

Where serious fictions are concerned, however, one thing at
    least is certain: to prate about Tolstoyan objectivity,
Portrayal of character, that sort of stuff, is to profess a lie.
It may be all right for lyric poets who are concerned with
    producing a merely poetic or pretty product to avoid
    looking into anything so tricky,
But the novelist, dramatist or narrative poet who pretends to
    know what goes on others' psychology:
He must look deep, deep into his own heart and then, O.K.,
    write.

THE GENERAL

Rapt in mere numerals of force, the child
Marching lead soldiers past an easy chair,
Will shrink into his nature from the wild
Animal slip and stagger of the fair:
Terrified when from his window perch he sees
Two tinkers fighting in the steaming air.

THE DECADENTS OF THE 1890S

The *nostalgie de la boue*
And unholy joy went together:
According to the loose assumptions anyway
They were birds of a single feather.

A notion which the lads encouraged:
Wine, sensuality and song,
While the gutter welcomed and the bloom fell early
Unto them they belonged.

And doubtless in the gutter quarter,
Where the poor were poorer still,
You could get what you wanted in the way of sinfulness
At a few bob a thrill.

For poverty, as we know, is relative
And the destitute sell what they have;
In a harsh world even some puzzled responses
Might be less than half a sov,

And a half a sov be riches
In the haunts where harlots were cheap,
Necessities weren't necessary
And girls grateful even for sleep.

But however the lads might sing of it,
Nymphs and nectar and lutes,
Instead of raw absinthe, disease and squalor
And poets like other brutes,

The truth is that as a Decadence
It couldn't compare with Up West,
Where the rich in their shining shirt-fronts
Wanted nothing but the Best,

Where everyone's health was looked after
And the thrill could be more prolonged,
And the roses went on blooming
Though flung riotously with the throng,

Where the wine-glasses sparkled like spangles
And nobody heard the lament
Of the pretty little waif who soon enough discovered
Precisely what Decadence meant.

And if the knowledge of this was somewhere
In the elegiac strain
Which ran through the hedonist verses
And spoke more of loss than of gain,

They had still, to prove that they weren't
Mere misfits, but self-condemned;
To go on singing of sin and pleasure
Doing them down in the end;

And in order to show the fitness
Of the fate that was in store
And épater the horrid bourgeois
Just that little bit more

Had to turn the grim attritions
Which are poverty's daily news,
The neglect and the dirty infections,
To distinctions choice spirits might choose;

And then to pretend that their dyings
Were satiated, jaded and just:
And the emptiness of existence
A surfeited life-disgust.

SOHO, FORTY EIGHT STREET AND POINTS WEST

On high gold heels that, perilous, hoist her forward with
    small heaves,
Actually lovely and not more than thirty,
Lashes like spider legs, a fleshy chin,
Eyes bright and blind as any desperate Star's
A smile that twitches at the messed up edges,
For, after all, she has a life elsewhere,
She spaces out with gloves and even bangles,
With theatre, the art so long to learn,
The allotted money span.
A sense of effort in these first gyrations,
A wobble in a turn, some shaky strides.
She too must have a hangover. Is this fair?
The rock beat is approved as for enjoyment
By all the world she knows and therefore proves
That this is show-biz too, class entertainment,
End of a girl's ambitions, once her gang's.
Enlarged banalities that echo small
Necessary realities of cloth and catch
Are needed to accomplish bareness.
With gestures which are public revenants
Of little automatic female ones,
Elbows triangles outward, fingers crooked
Between her shoulder blades as she unhooks
Her brassiere, an afternoon reminder
Of many furnished rooms in when she throws
A stocking towards a couch and it won't get there,
She steps out of the ordinary mesh
To be to drumbeats only, to begin
The long and leisured insult which her surface,
The independent acreage of her skin
Swops with these still observers.
Alone, alone, for she is all alone,
The ritual victim while the other girls
Sit round backstage and smoke, she's now the one,
And bare to storms of stares, a mere forked animal,
Endures incomprehensibles and smiles.
It is a state. A form of theatre in each buttock's crease.
Lifting her jellied vulnerable breasts

(The female mammal is a beast of burden)
She leans towards each, suggests conspiracy,
The secret compact with the opposite sex.
It isn't on. The front row glowers back sternly,
Yields to such blandishments a bleak rebuke.
We men have spent our lives in pleasing too.
There's no need now to simulate response:
Here he who pays the stripper calls the tune.
Her bottom, blue beneath the powder, carried
Around the stage and individually offered
As apes do to us all to prove submission,
She lies down while the drum beats rock to climax
To incur the final shame.
In semblance of an ecstasy begins,
Legs thrashing, long hair spread and bitten, murmuring
(Priapus hangs his head and it's reproved)
To steal one more prerogative from the male,
In rapture rolling there before some strangers
Whom she admits to this, the last exclusion.
In the long war they wage with one another
She whom the rock beat mocks, the repetition,
The money, masculine, its obscure purpose,
And they, the once romantics, once rejected,
Both by financial compact here are victors,
For they, who have paid, the masters, take on her,
As she, whose flesh is palpable, takes on them,
An indifferent but clawing sweet revenge.

THE MIDDLE YEARS

These are the middle years,
The years of aggrandisement, when
The big philosophical question
Seems not to need any answer.
This is what it's about,
Youth's gaucheries survived,
The missus and he in accord,
The new Jag in the garage,
The odd bit on the side.
Now life justifies itself,
The strong grip on the racquet,
A firm hand on the gears,
Confidence worn like a suit,
The memorable weekend
With that real wild Danish piece.
The kids making eager choices
Are nearly enough to provide
Sufficient purpose in living:
By God, that's a clever lad!
An actuary! Think of that!
If you can stretch them out,
Still fit and trim enough,
A secretary's dream,
The bugbear what's it about
Is successfully postponed
Even for those who, well ...
Still go to mass of course.
Stretch them out further still
It might even seem to vanish.

MORTAL CONFLICTS

The people of the opaque screens glow with a frenzy of
  motive,
Are haloed by purpose and rage as they stalk across the hotel
  lobbies
In gloves and dark glasses committing well-plotted murders
For money, or power, out of love, or anyway, let's admit,
  passion
They attempt at least to take charge of their star's portion
And die out their lives in an ecstasy of calculation.
And so when they lose to the law and laconic detectives have
  spoken
They have as their epitaphs anyway the disturbances and the
  closures.

The people of the little parlours are on the other hand passive,
Sitting in the pebble-dashed house that they put their name
  on a list for
Among neighbours they don't really like, at weekends they
  see their relations.
They plug on at the job they're lucky to have and will until
  they're redundant.
The sweet evenings gone they suffer the ever after,
The big choice of the year being Benidorm or Majorca.
And if there's a dust-up or sudden outcrop of tragedy
It's more often than not because some fool had a few drinks
  too many one night.

The people of the acclaimed masterpieces are concerned with
  moral problems
Or with happiness or fulfilment or the affiancing of properties
And when as they will these things conflict great battles are
  fought in the psyche
As well as in fact. They hasten by Pullman or droshky
To confrontations in country houses, in lawyers' offices, at
  soirées,
Are stern in their purposed outfacings and sterner still in their
  partings.
Moving to meet their fate with intent and leaving their girls
  by the lakeside.

No wonder that when it's all over we have a sense of
  catharsis.

But the reader engrossed in such reachings for life possibility
Reaches for nothing. It comes to him through the letter box.
The family car gets larger then smaller again as the years pass.
The girl in accounts goes away, he doesn't write back to her.
He notices drift when reminded by others about
  anniversaries
And finds he has burned his boats when rummaging
  somewhere for cigarettes.
His conflicts are mortal merely and without much moral
  significance.

NO LONGER TRUE ABOUT TYRANTS

The popular notion of the tyrant should be of someone
Who, suddenly assailed, as we may all be suddenly assailed,
By the ruched blouse stretched across the breasts, by the knees
 or the entrancing smile
Of the popular domestic science student whom the
 municipality and her fellow pupils
Had deputed to present him with flowers, says brusquely
To the arranger who is always at his side, anxious to arrange
 such,
Have that one sent to the Schloss tonight, God how I love it.
Or at the ballet at the end of a tiring day
(And how wearisome the ballet itself can be for the tired
 spectators
Except for the sweet things with their kohl-deep eyes across
 the footlights),
Being suddenly anguished, as lesser mortals may equally be
 anguished,
Says, bring me the dark-haired one in the second row
Who looks as if she might have come from the Lower
 Provinces,
And even though brought the wrong, incidentally Jewish, one
 is so impatient
He commands her to lie down in the dim lit box in the empty
 echoing theatre.
Or else it should be of the tyrant as an epicure who after four
 full courses with the stuffy ambassadors
Says, I feel like a light repast with my two as of now trusted
 cronies,
And proceeds behind locked doors to the light repast room
Where the kneeling girls naked except for thin collars and
 chains serve, serve,
Until one of them eats him, nibbling very slowly as she has
 been instructed.

But alas for this idea of the tyrant it is not so.
It is not even remotely like. It is considerably less human.
The tyrant is actually one who with millions of pairs of breasts
 and buttocks at his disposal
Confines himself to boring Eva Braun with her bourgeois tea
 parties.

There are newsreels of Hitler inspecting rows of blonde
  mädchen in singlets,
Bare shoulders back, breasts forward, eyes right adoring,
All of whom have been bent and swayed to his evil purposes
And could be bent and swayed again at a twitch of his
  swagger stick,
But are not bent or swayed either because he is too moral,
Too careful of his image in the eyes of the multitude and
  afraid of rumour,
Even mention of glassy-eyed Eva Braun being forbidden for
  fear of scandal,
Or whose appetite is simply for paper, paper
Showing how many human forms have disappeared into his
  abyss,
His supporters in so far as they want to know being
  convinced that they are enemies,
How many millions of people, whether personable, male or
  female
Have been placed at the disposal of the state, have been
  stripped and beaten
Without anybody above the rank of master sergeant or clerk
  fourth grade,
Who can hardly be said to be men of power, even having an
  erection,
The rest being perfect models of the bureaucracy or cogs in a
  machine
Which like its master is bafflingly incapable of seizing its
  opportunities.
Whatever we were told in the tales of Bluebeard it is not so.
The really great bullies are more up tight, more respectable or
  more calculating even than the rest of us.
Poor suffering, slavering humanity does not even get the
  tyrants it so richly deserves.

LA DIFFERENCE

Monsieur Junot,
Late, partly, of the Palace, Monaco,
Told journalists,
"All is over between Caroline and me.
We are both free
To do as we please."
But Mister Bruno
Of 84 Bloomfield Avenue
Is not in that category.
He has left it too late.
When he goes even for a pint
The garden gate
Clungs behind him with the clung of fate.
Although in its various forms unease
Is the most constant emotion he feels with Missus Bruno
Neither are free to do as they please.
Unlike Monsieur Junot,
Mister Bruno
Cannot afford "a period of separation"
Or a pad of his own in the Rue De L'Amour.
He is consumed by avoidance of periods of desperation
And the demands of Number 84.
Nor, even if the opportunity
Should offer, could he go
"On holiday in Turkey
With a red-haired young woman
Described as his secretary."
On all but four weeks of the year,
Likewise devoted to the family,
He has to go to workey.
And yet all, you know,
Really is over between him and Missus Bruno.
For one thing
Mister Bruno
Has acquired the habit of stroving,
Which might be described
As a careful correlation
Of a sort of striving
With a sort of loving
And even a sort of affectionate patting and stroking.

And by no stretch of the imagination
Or anything else
Can a strover
Turn back into a lover.
Yet this habit goes deep, deep:
Deeper even than the others
To which Mister Bruno is addicted,
Deeper even than the smoking
Of fifty fags a day.
But whatever about Mister Bruno,
Monsieur Junot
Is unlikely to acquire the habit
Or know the little joys
Of stroving.
As to which is the more fortunate?
You must be joking.

SINE QUA NON

Nearly all that is good,
Almost all that is ease,
And, if there were revelations,
Even, perhaps, these.

The appointed hours of discovery
Which will never again wait
Across some sunlit courtyard
And through some welcoming gate;

Delighted converse of equals
Who have nothing to lose or gain
Arrangements made or decided,
A bed for the night or a train;

Freedom to manage mere circumstance
After the first held glance,
Lamplit, islanded evenings
And the full answering sense;

A long longed-for abandonment
To the far blue over rock,
In that landscape's being
Still the immersion shock;

Yes, nearly all that is good,
Very nearly all that is truth,
Now, in the middle way,
As in entangled youth:

Witnessing, touching, partaking,
The mere presence at the spot,
Mostly functions of money,
The without which, not.

And, at the end of it all,
With or without grace,
The funeral too a function
And whether it takes place.

RETURNED YANK

When Tim O'Dowd's father died,
Dead broke,
In a room in Dorset Street in Dublin,
After the local woman had laid him out
(It had to be decent)
Tim was left alone with the old man's body
(There had to be some sort of wake).
Because the old legs were too long for the sheets
The feet stuck out at the end, and,
Looking at them,
Timothy thought of the miles those feet had walked:
Looking for jobs,
Looking for lodgings,
Looking for company,
Up and down stairs,
In and out of bars,
Bars on the Bowery,
Bars in Dublin,
Miles on the beat even
For he had been a cop
In "little old New York",
"Got the boot for drink",
Looking for his wife
Who went off with someone else
After five years in the States –

On the pavements of two worlds those calloused feet

Walked their weary,
Remorseful,
Anxious,
EVEN EAGER
Miles.

To what avail?
Only themselves were testimony now.

COMPLETION

All things tend to completion,
Towards a resultant end.
The heat of a harvest noonday
With an August night will blend.

The rose burns out in its calyx.
The leaf yields to the ground.
Almost every appearance
Is with disappearance crowned.

CONCORD

Sweeter to be the master, says the master.

Sweeter to be the instrument, the instrument is crying
In delightful apprehension as he nears.

Sweeter to be the instrument, oh sweeter far
The passionate instrument cries to the dominant master,
As all its withinness lingers before release.

Oh but sweeter to be the releaser of this answer,
This sentience that is greater, he avers,
As his tangled self is uttered by its truth.

The instrument, the master, beguiled by the one passion,
Become master, instrument now of the same articulation.

Sweeter to be the master, cries the world.

LAST RITES

As death forecloses further possibility, the priest anoints each sense, the point of that perception and its mode, asking forgiveness for what sins occurred through being the possessor of those senses, having:

Sight

This was the open one, instantly, encompassing flight and line, bulk and concavity, block and recession, and finding in everything that could be encompassed, relationship, order and balance. Nor were divorce and separation from the object a bar to this delight. Beyond contact or embrace, through this you have known surface and shape. Beyond savour, essence.

But rejecting seeing you sought often another sort of dominion; and, yearning for what was properly beyond reach, conditioned yourself to a relative rather than an absolute.

For, transcending sight, you could only attempt to possess.

Smell

This was the traveller. This was the one which made all prompt with knowledge of the strange, which said how clean the desert air, how fecund in possibility the riverside streets, and in which direction the sea.

But this was the rememberer also. If you had always been aware of this you would not have believed it was so easy to escape, for this would have reminded you again and again of the redolent, inevitable cycle, ending you know where and in what.

And it was as much as anything else the avoidance of odours which helped you to entertain the old idealist dream, from which all must awake, though some not before it is too late.

Hearing

Without sounds, delectable in themselves, you would not have sought always to be closer to the source. If something had not been heard, you would not have sought to hear more clearly still that word of comradeship or that word of love.

Without report, rumour and gossip yeah you would have

rested content, not knowing the wonderful mediations of envy and ambition, nor framing your life-giving definitions of enemy and friend.

But by denying what was heard you condemned yourself to the special torments of those who are not only unhappy, but believe themselves to be unique as well, and to their special unnecessary heroism, which isolates still further.

Taste

Without it you would never have known that acceptance of whatever is near at hand need not be a confession of failure but a source of settled joy. You would not have experienced the love of opposites, or the equal attraction of two extremes, known why we must not disdain the seemingly unfitted, nor discovered of what unlikely ingredients the good is nearly always compounded.

And if through love of what was mixed, blended and watered down you sometimes found the way but lost the truth, were led to worship the subtleties of the dialectic and began to believe in the happy medium.

Nevertheless it was by neglecting this that you allowed yourself to believe that a part might be the whole and began to exalt single categories over all others.

Touch

This was the liberator. Without this you would have remained in thrall to the sterile prodigies of the imagination, and thus never experience the rich complexities of a world where what appears to be is related to what is, accident to ultimate essence, the gleaming manifestation to the dark inner substance.

And conversely, it was through this that you came to understand that the veil may not be a disguise merely but itself a revelation, that the texture can be all there is to know and the surface the ultimate reality.

This was, then, the best proof of existence: your own, and, more important perhaps, that of the entelechies which were the whole matter of your rejoicing. And in so far as you ignored or disregarded this, as you did them all, this was the sense worst starved.

IN PRAISE OF CONSTRICTION

Who does not dream of direct utterance, free of the fictive
    web
Or the rhyme's restrictions,
Even of the described circumstance,
The embodiment,
Which damnably always pertains
To mere attractiveness, texturization,
The exotic or picturesque,

Who, that is, that has a truth to say,
Or a cry to make from the heart?
Herman Melville declared
That in place of those elaborate constructions
Which are the plays of Shakespeare
With their scenes to be filled out and coincidences managed,
Poisoned sword-tips and discovered letters,
He had always yearned to hear
The still, rich utterance
Of that great soul
In full repose.
And yet he himself
In setting his ship to sea
And manning it
And stocking the great ocean,
Not just in memory of all those wide-skied days
And the freedom of voyages and waters,
Nor even as a celebration of necessity,
Men going about their work
As they do go about their work, out of economic need,
Or loyalty to those they call their loved ones,
Killing and flaying, knee-deep in blubber and shit,
But also as a story with a beginning and an end,
A something that never was, no more than Queequeg or
    Ahab,
No more than the white whale,
Came during that fiction and that foundering
Upon so many truths and even their substantiation,
The rest, without that adventure,
That, if you like sea story,
Being indeed a silence.

And the obstacles to free, plain speech are in fact enormous
Because not there.
If there are no constricting channels through which to flow,
As through Diego's ground the sparkling torrent passed,
Bringing the green shoots up
On his day for the water,
It all spreads out,
Runs silver thin and then
Disappears through the thirsty ground.

Story form, with its predestined meetings,
Partings, dooms, its impositions
Even of motive, perhaps, and outcomes anyway:
Substantive form,
The syllable count,
The sonnet's narrow cell,
Both constrictive,
A pattern imposed, on the fluidities
Of the material, life-experience;
Or the material, which is also, of course, words.
Both narrowings,
But somehow making possible
An area of cultivation
In the otherwise dismaying and defeating expanse.
In searching for the rhyme you find the truth
Which up to that point had eluded
Not the mere saying, but the realization.
In following the story through with its accretions
You came to the situation
Which unlocks what was within
And are suddenly possessed of the insight which has already
    yours;
Or you come upon the image
Which has waited for place and context
Disturbing heart and sense
Dumbly and pointlessly for twenty years.

Of course the pre-ordained myths
Have burdens of their own,
For which see Campbell, Tucker, Kirk and other estimable
    savants,
But humbler stories

Such as Shakespeare's stolen plots
Or the thirty (?) famous basics;
Even, supposing you have that sort of talent,
Something invented, though, as Edith said,
"Invention is the enemy
of all the arts",
May still have use as mere conveyance,
Bringing us at last to the places ... well, that mattered,
Where the driveway began, the gatekeeper's cottage
And the almost silent mill emitted its puffs of steam;
Or, say, the suburb where the tramlines ended
In a country road with vineyards
And the harsh blue and red Cinzano stencil
Peeled from the café gable.
To put it crudely,
In the fiction
The protagonist comes to the place where the poet has been.
During the voyage between the islands, in the endless rain
The oil smell and the sea smell meet as they did at the ships'
    stairhead.

It depends of course on what you are after.
There are the valid images of event,
What we were looking at, what we saw
At some point in time when an imprint was left on the
    memory, psyche or spirit
For which somehow the words timeless or even immortal
Seem not implausible;
The place in Antonio's lane where the outhouse wall began
And a girl in a T-shirt waited on a bicycle, balancing,
One arm outstretched,
Though this was scarcely an event as most story-tellers
understand event,
Clearly and immediately causative or resultant.
And then there are those images which find for some
unknown reason a respondent
In the innermost self,
Somehow outside time altogether and
Scarcely connected with other emotion or event at all,
More like communion than reflection or debate:
The dilapidated barn among the olive trees,
Coarse sun-absorbent brick, slits squeezed against the glare.

But alas in most stories, in the novel of the month,
Setting is merely convenient location for the action,
Because what happens has to happen somewhere,
In the hotel lobby,
The airport lounge,
On the cathedral steps
And objects are merely stage properties serving the purposes
    of the plot,
The shotgun on the wall which will go off in the third act,
Not images with their own entelechy,
Like a child's toy,
Or the intensity of those which made up of the mise en scène
For the real, agonising turning point,
When things were decided, one way or another,
Or were not decided, the images haunting unappeased.
Which is to say nothing either of the rooted,
Ingrowing images of home and habit
Among which nothing happens
That could conceivably claim the status of the revelations of
    narrative.
Between the window and the door we sit.
The ghosts are elsewhere, where the rocking lights
Sway above swaying waves,
A water tinged with neon as with blood.

Nevertheless, a fiction or at least a narrative may be necessary
With its gearings, descriptions, destinations
So that we may come to the point where the true images can
    re-exist
Or even come to the crucial event.
One writes a story
In order to come to a hallstand, a fountain or a change of
    heart:
Fabricates a construction
In order to come to a meeting in the deserted
Plaza de los Reyes, and an implausible kiss.
In the strange southern city
Where our hero has now arrived
The drain smell hangs in the street
And we can set down again
And exorcise, redeem or explain,
Something of the ecstasy, something of the shame.

And because of the story's turning
One finds also one's truths.
As the ship interminably edges up to the dock
And the diesel smell thickens
The donkey engine whining and stopping
He discovers the meaning of home.

It is a question of embodiment, yes,
But also of mere utterance,
For the naming otherwise,
The mere naming, or the direct statement
Of the truth we know,
Lacking context and its immediate, well, inspiration,
May somehow never, whatever its urgency, come to pass
And be lost in the life-noises of a smoky suburb.
A brick simply a brick and a lath a lath
Lying on the ground unless the total structure
Calls for a reaching out.
The needs, the direction of the fiction decide not the truth to
    be said,
But whether it is said.

And the myth or even the humbler fiction may provide too,
At last perhaps and after long waiting
The locus round which those images will gather
Which have unknown affinities,
So that, yes, hearing the typewriter, smelling the roses,
In fact the patio's geraniums,
The white gloved guardia leading the religious procession
And the stumpy biplane at the airfield's edge
Become part of the single experience,
The petroleum smell of the fly-killer,
The prism of the raindrop
And the sense of loss in the pale evening
Reveal their significance in relation to each other.
For images, needing a myth or a structure to have their being
    in
Are like ghosts which need houses,
A habitation where men go about their business,
Not seeming to care.
And for the contemporary world
With all its discordance

And apparent meaninglessness,
The two-stroke engines in the street below,
The endless revving and hooting adding to the heat,
The flies attracted to the market fish;
And after dark
The drugged whores by the canal bank
Their thighs white in the headlights as the males make their
    nightlong inspection,
The skyscraper filling the water,
A couple at a café table reading Neruda together, their heads
    touching;
Canary cages in the slums
And anarchist slogans on the cathedral wall
No votez sin libertad;
The luck is to find the magnetis lithos,
The focal point in the night round which such images will
    gather,
The great ship with its lights shining on absolute blackness,
And gathering round that city-like thing,
Calamity or newsflash,
Which has affinities for all
Discover affinities for themselves.
The luck would have been of course
For the letter not to have been delivered
And a decision made which had something to do with duty,
    law,
Work, worry, the inability to face pain, one's own or an
    other's,
Or perhaps, strange to say, the absence of passion,
To be not alone in the great meaningless city
With the tannery stink on the one side,
The fish-market smells on the other,
The little three-wheeler vans in the traffic jam always outside
And the sunlight through the slats of the shutters
Waking one to absence, humanity going about its business
And in the cafés as well as in the galleries,
Envy of lovers, perhaps the worst disease.

Yet there are images which stand alone …

And how, story or myth apart,
In poems too

A mere theme pursued,
An "argument" in the other sense,
May, line by line, reveal
Lost poems, truths or lost occasions, images
In search of home, a "love poem" be
Many poems, which may be as much about
Separation and distance, a southern city
Shuttered against the heat,
Men and women going about their business,
As they do go,
The fear of incurring or of giving pain,
Perhaps, strange to think, lack of passion,
And what we call necessity, duty, or the law as love.

THE END OF THE MODERN WORLD
(1989)

for Dermot Bolger

I

1.
The clinging, clayey soils of our wet north
Defeated Roman farmers and the rain
Which swept in from the west made swamps of fen
Until the mould-board plough dragged through the mud
By wretched rows of oxen tied together
Raised ridges in the worst of fields, the flattest,
Which drained the water from the land. The low-skied
North then found the rain a virtue. Twice a year,
Both in the quickening showers of Spring and later,
In that queer stillness of a clear October
When Autumn gutters out behind the trees,
Ploughs could be run. This haunted north, more fertile
Than ever the ghost-free south, gave forth a surplus
Which fed new ghosts, great visions, dreams, desirings.

2.
But first the fields had to expand, the manor
Lord had to make the laws which marked out strips,
Long, narrow, straight, for cultivation by
The teams of beasts which they now yoked and shared.
Loving the bounds that soon were set to nature,
What tilth and pasture, path and orchard are,
The russet wall absorbing sun in summer,
The embracing firelight of the hall in winter
To forest folk who dread return of danger,
Gloating on barn and mill, they daily, gladly
Gave up their own dream to that dream, the stronger,
Whose bridle twitch was terror to the farmer
But struck into his soul, sweet compensation,
Love of a safe, harsh, iron domination.

3.

The grain soared upward into golden arches,
Transmuted into groined and pointed stone,
Miraculous vaulting, delicate great defiance
Of all the laws of earth; and men aspiring
To something better than law, beyond condition,
Tithe and toll, their poor bowed psyches soaring
Among these upward arches from the ground
Mingled with angels in melodious heights.
Other immortals had been at home on earth,
Bathed in rivers, hunted woods, chased girls
With womb and orifice, weak and wet to touch.
Now tempted to transcendence men became
Half angels, monsters, who were soon to learn
How half-men hate the bodies which they mourn.

4.

Following the curve of arches, like a fountain,
The music of the mingled voices rose,
Seeming spontaneous, pure detached emotion.
The schemings that his fellows called ambition,
Conspiracies which served what passed for passion,
Furtive arrangements while with straight hair falling
Over his brow and level eyebrows, laughing
The loved one walked another line but knew him
Still for friend, lost in this soaring.
It seems to boys that spirit is a kingdom
Whose law is feeling, meeting like the arches.
They little know how marvellous calculation
Through which both note and arch meet in dependence.
But they will learn, and learn they were mistaken.

5.
Keeping his vigil nightlong in the chancel,
Seeing a vision of himself resplendent
Beside what gave him caste, his murderous weapons,
The always brave, the honourable one,
Sans peur et sans reproche, sought echo answer
From something guiltless, sin-free but still human,
A virgin merging in her slender girlhood
With all which was appointed to confirm him
In his ideal of him. And as he knelt there
The hope grew unassuagable at last
Except by one so far above her fellows
That she could not be found, or, if found, taken,
Allow the peaks and valleys of her body
To be the territory of his hands.
Thus forfeited their friendship and their love.

6.
Leaving aside then for all time the songs
So wonderfully waiting to be sung
On that lost, long, tolling Sunday when he knew
So well the infinite bitterness of being young;
Leaving out break of cloud and depth of sky,
The green of water in a wooded place,
The answering curve of the always indomitable
Blood towards body's grace;
Leaving for ever out of dream and living
The beauty of the gravely mocking face;
What else remains to be remembered,
Or ever for time's remembrance to be said,
Before on the homely pillow of white death
He lays his tired with longing, mortal head?

7.

He rode to war along the rime-rimmed roads,
Awaiting wounds to prove his love for her,
His horse hooves splitting ice like sparkling stars.
And she was present like the evening star,
Like god or conscience, knowing all he did,
And he spoke nightly of his deeds to her,
Who saw him, careless, brave and generous,
As he, a hero in his own song, saw;
Who trembled for his daring as he dashed
Forward where danger was and all but death.
And in this docile comradeship of hers,
Worshipping lance and badge and saddle straightness,
He found more than he would find, coming home
To that passivity he had wished upon her.

8.

But in that longing sweetness greater than
The sweetness sex released into the blood
When he rode south to Barbary where girls
Hung ripe as fruit and palpable and many.
Her absent presence was as light as air,
Like fountain spray, blown suddenly to stroke,
An amulet, a password or a charm.
So that when he returned and she was given
Unbrided, a mere mortal in the house,
An animal in bed, kind, egocentric,
No centre but periphery of space,
Aching for absence still he sought another
Whose beauty would be hedged by swords and forests
So the keen longing would go on forever.

9.
The arming and departure of the knights:
A picture by Burne-Jones in Birmingham.
The armourers are maidens clothed in white,
Cool draperies denying horse-hot limbs.
They raise their lashes to their lads, the knights,
Are almost bold in promise as they hand
The spear and shield, the sword and helmet up
That when he comes back, glory work all done,
The union he will find will be complete,
Demure but total, ending adolescent
Agonies, new manhood's long self doubtings,
Weakness acknowledging its opposite,
For strength reserving servile adoration:
Burne-Jones, a man, is painting a male dream.

10.
In the long fields he saw the woman crawl,
Hoeing and snagging, buttocks high, and took them
In that position when the steward brought them,
Naked of woollen cloth and washed as never
Since their day of birth in smoky cabins,
Blushing like roses or like russet apples.
Como un perro, laughed and forced his member
Between the labia, the strong thrust driving
The head turned sideways, hair in disarray,
Among the rushes of the castle chamber.
Looking along the plane of back, the neck bared,
Saw just enough of face to savour dominance.
Como un perro. But it was the human
Against which he blasphemed, and not the animal.

11.
And when they knelt before him, took his member
Between their lips, their lashes low, allowing
Unquestioning prerogative, he suffered
Division in his heart. No ruler ever,
No owner of the women in the woods
While making free in search of his own pleasure
Dreamed girlhood set so strangely high above him,
So wished its blinding snows immaculate.
Torn thus could not find his delight with equals,
Dismayed by women of the kitchen aching
With lust just like his own, but liberal, human,
Preferred to dominate and found instead
Intoxication stranger and much stronger
In knowing it was always an offence.

12.
The king sits, you will notice, fully armoured,
Impregnable in iron, while the maid
Is wearing just a shift or flimsy nightdress
Which clings to belly curve and even navel,
Shining like, oddly, some post-war synthetic,
Her arms and shoulders very white and bare.
She's almost on an altar, perched above him,
He's practically kneeling down below,
Taking a good long look. Her gaze is fixed
On the wall behind him and above his head.
(Some never look at all at the front rows.)
"The meaning of it has been much debated."
The female is a goddess to be worshipped.
Also an object you can sit and look at.

13.
Lady Burne-Jones thought that "Cophetua"
Showed the special qualities of her husband's art
Better than anything else he ever painted.
Certainly steps and throne are deeply pleasing
In their recessive quality at least.
It's said the girl is a Miss Francis Graham,
With whom he was in love, but who got married.
He's "gazing at her in mute admiration."
He had that curious garment specially made
And posed another model in it too.
The grave, sad face of course is still Miss Graham's.
That dear one can be worshipped like an icon
And placed, a precious object, on a shelf.
The shift reveals though. Equally the armour.

14.
The heather gives off sweetness in the warm
Impulsive air and over it hangs bee song
Like a cloud. Below, bright yellow furze
Crumbles dry rock; then the rich grass begins.
A river rubs its way past small clay cliffs
And inlets where sleek cattle sniff the water.
A silver bell is tolling. Holy men
Murmur a chant like bees. In outhouses
The women knead the bread, their creamy thoughts
Curl gently at the edges like the dough.
There is no history here, the hurt who make it
Banished to knife-sharp islands where they punish
Their sex for its impossible demands,
Rejections of this possible content.

15.

An air which softens outlines, blurs horizons,
Hides mountain ranges until suddenly
The black peaks soar, steep, huge and sodden over
A valley where the stream and road are one.
In this land nothing's clear, no colour sharp
Except the green. The browns and reds and purples
Change constantly and quickly with the moisture
Content of the air, as does the light.
The twilight lingers, bright but shadowless
Beyond the sunset. Since the sea surrounds
The whole, east light and west, north light and south
Are at the mercy of its mirror mass.
The south is sometimes clearer than the north
And ambiguity a law of life.

16.

The chief a hero and the herd boy kinsman
Hung on his gestures, watched his debonair
Way with a sword hilt, eagerly crouched and honoured
His hunter's empathy with the hillside's life.
And when the clan was summoned to the sign,
The high notes swelling in sweet auguries
Of fellowship and sacrifice, he followed
Until the day when all was lost and loyalty
Became the only riches to be shared.
He sat all night beside the sleeping form,
Lochiel wrapped in his cloak, his blonde, damp, royal
Hair on the heather's pillow. In the boy's full heart
A gratitude for service greater than
The systems know, or women, or even knowledge.

17.
Connolly wrote that all was held in common,
That everyone was equal in the clan,
Copying Mrs Alice Stopford Green,
As did the whole intoxicated crew.
There was no competition. None could fail.
For boys confirmed what Scott and Stevenson
Had said of something other than a world
In which each little family looked out
From narrow windows on their enemies,
Plotting advantage like conspirators.
MacNeill put a stop to that in 1912,
Gave Russell a breakdown, upset the rest.
MacNeill, "that traitor", but a scholar too.
All scholarship is perhaps a kind of treason.

18.
Such lived by litheness, by the quick reflex,
The lunge and limit of the lovely claw,
So lazy but so terrible in stroke,
Their tawniness the only value known
Until the law, an awe-struck lover, gave
The sanction of the temple and the grove,
The exactitudes of language and its grace
To pre-existing power and privilege.
They now had all, arched foot and architecture,
The woods within whose wildness they still hunted,
The earth which they had seized and wedded like
A cataclysm in the long ago.
So more than natural seemed, so weak they were,
Surpassing nature, ignorant of its ways,
And ignorant too of number, interest.

19.
And suddenly their limbs grew weak, their weapons
Awkward and wayward in their gauche right hands.
From the smoke-shrouded city which had sheltered
So much that was unmentionable: plague,
Curiosity, measurement, foreign women,
Emerged a strange miasma, whose effect
On them was as infection, though the ones
About whom like a magic or a cloud
It hung, seemed unaffected, even strengthened.
When such came with this aura and calm eyes
Ancient woods withered at the very root,
The land, their bride, turned alien and cold.
Strange mist which tainted all that they thought good
And yet enhanced too everything men owned.

20.
More shocking than the westward sea being blocked,
The discovery that all was now for sale.
Many had understood how brutish power
Could overbear, entrap the bright and brave,
Bring the slight trembling virgin to the bed,
Send statuary crashing to the ground,
Reduce the Lord's anointed to a wretch
Pleading for pardon or a sup of water.
Still there was honour, which could be lost, suborned,
But not sold like a chattel to another,
Fidelity, forever a fixed star,
Entitlement, a wine within the blood,
And field and wood entailed to son and heir.
Strange they should think the sale of these the worst.

21.
Le Roi Soleil, the great sun burning down
On all his subjects, brought a sort of light.
He cut the finest figure in the world
On his high heels with ribbons at his knees.
And he built nobly too. The oxen dragged
Long carts through rutted clay, boards buckling under
Huge blocks of stone until the architect's
Conception rose, baroque and beautiful.
All this was quite gratuitous, a fountain
Is not a dour necessity of state;
And though the powerful hydraulic pumps
Which he commissioned are still marvels, they
Were not employed except in the king's gardens.
So those free from necessity invent.

22.
The boredom was extreme, the lack of privacy
Unbearable. He went to bed in public
And ate his breakfast under the crowd's stare.
The closet lined with books and ledgers, sex
Like a shameful contract between two,
These were inventions of the bourgeoisie.
They played cards endlessly, intrigued and gossiped,
Screaming inside with rage like idle children,
Hour after hour, talk, talk; and, worse still, wit.
Gallantry was a task required, exacted.
And only war provided work of import
Almost as stern as that the bourgeois did.
"O Richard, o mon roi", the royalists
Would sing, invoking sweet recovered dangers.

23.
The great Crown was surmounted by a Cross.
The judge twitched ermine and adjusted scarlet.
The archbishop's purple matched his purple lips.
Insignia and symbol proved the man
Himself but instrument, though with a taste
For blood, or boys, or beauties kept like deer
Within a park. The mob outside the gates
Saw symbol first; of god's power greater than
The human office, but that greater than
The mortal man who filled it. Blows at this
Struck at the ceremony of the universe,
Stars in melodic courses, high on high,
Not at poor privilege, thin-shanked and trembling,
Keeping with fear his darlings, strange as deer.

24.
The classic portico confronts the lake
Flung like a challenge to its very steps.
The inspirational, instinctual,
Flees like the deer to forest and green fern.
We put our trust in clearer definition,
Contract and construct, law and well marked limit,
Reason proclaiming all mankind was one,
Its interests symmetrical and known,
The set square, T square and dividers could
Map out its future on a drawing board.
Masters who made possession the sole order
Twisted the reasoning. Rebellious, sullen,
Native to darkness now, the instincts gathered,
Hate in their hearts and hateful in their turn.

25.
O blessed fruits of hate, unthinking hate,
Unknowing, without theory or even
Without cause, the smouldering, sullen hate
Of peasants grimed from birth, grimed in the bone,
Who know themselves inferior for ever
Who can never even stroll like him in gardens,
Never be free in body or with bodies,
Or pause like him at the apex of the dance.
Hate the last holy, inextinguishable
Prerogative of those too cowardly
Ever to strike a blow, who shamble by
In humble silence while the horsemen pass,
Their secret flame, their pledge and proud distinction,
Their sole assertion of an opposite state.

26.
Their ancestors were wise, they dug and trenched,
Plumbing foundations in the quaking soil.
Raising the chaste, severe and classical
Column, entablature and pediment,
Reproving nature with proportion's stare
And showing man a measurer for joy.
So let stand thus forever stylobate,
Podium, portico and colonnade,
Organic artlessness acknowledged in
The thin acanthus leaf but now transcended.
Who tumbles, burns or tarnishes beware
How rare is balance, brought about in mass,
Rightness which none can rectify, dispute,
The threatened made enduring, lines in air.

27.
But strike they did and threw a king's cropped head
As gage of battle to the kings of Europe,
Thus horrifying many gentle souls.
And Erba said, a far day to remember,
Walking beside Max Reinhardt's urns and columns,
Two suns, the second broken on the water,
Schloss Leopold, the joy of the baroque,
A tracery across the darker side,
No Barbara that day; "Unhappiness
Came into Europe with that revolution
As mode where only misery had been."
Through thirty years quite clear, two poets in amber.
Now after all those years I find the answer:
No, not unhappiness but discontent.

28.
Sweet Liberty enthroned in Notre Dame,
A smudged girl, carmined, licking nervous lips.
The wits joked, as she tremulously mounted,
Her lath and plaster eminence of mounts
And the innumerable clients who had climbed them.
Thus Liberty and Whoredom rose together
And have been quite inseparable since,
Freedom to prostitute themselves enjoyed
By talented persons in all walks of life
And money able to command young minds,
Their willingness, their grace, their sober virtue.
Contract instead of status it's been called.
Executives in Saabs who know their worth,
Smarter of course than other kinds of whore.

29.
And Emmet said, his voice a dulcet tenor,
"I placed a time bomb under the Free State,
It was one of my sneered-at technical devices,
My exploding cobble-stones and signal rockets,
'When my country takes her place among the nations,
Then and not till then ...' You know the gist.
They cut off my head when they cut me up in Thomas Street,
A mess of offal, thrown to political dogs,
Yet I had been clever for once, in spite of my blunders.
Cosgrave at mass in a morning coat, winged collar,
Could hear beyond the coughing and the gabble
The beat of a Jacobin drum. We were both politicians.
Is it not the Jacobin dream that is scrawled in the jakes:
'Up the Republic. Up the IRA.'?

30.
"They dragged the Lord Chief Justice from his coach,
A mottled and blanched old man who loved his grandchild.
This has been held against me ever since
Alike by those who say, what is, is right,
And those who say what is not should remain
With unstained annals until it becomes
The true republic, Roman, rational.
My superbly folded stock and flowered waistcoat,
The justice and humanity of my cause,
My acquaintance with the works of Paine and Rousseau,
Worthless, in face of this. Yet this was progress.
Your other sad rebellions had been raised
For rural reasons. Mine at least was modern.
My mob was European, avant-garde.

31.
"I was ignorant of tribal rights and wrongs,
Sad wranglings over scrub and bog, the rival
Interpretation of the books of wrath,
And cared not much for nations either except
As communes with accountable delegates.
Doubtless, though, many who followed me may have wanted
Some sort of mystic justice or reversal,
To see a fine old gentleman shitting his breeches
And hear him cry for absent law and order.
Of course there were human passions outside my range.
They were not all on the level of dreamy Dowdall,
Quigley the bricklayer, learned Stafford the baker,
But I took what was to hand in the real world,
The hatreds it creates, its judges foster."

32.
Almost as if they had a horror of
The things we find consoling to the spirit,
The rook-filled trees around the rectory,
The restless sighing of the captive leaves,
The river's ceaseless conflict with the stones,
The weeping cattle, clustered at the gate,
And the rich fields, the rippling flanks of earth,
They fled their rose-embowered dwellings for
The deserts of uprooting, a new landscape,
Poisoned, where nothing grew and even sky
Was man-made, black as coal, where, hope abandoned,
Of any sign that what they saw intended
A destiny for them in harmony
With nature, they now thronged through factory gates.

33.

But nature too had now been touched by man,
Its very root and branch, each berry, tuber,
The shining blades of grass, the bleating sheep
Who spread like an infection through the vales,
The golden ears of corn, which, bursting through
Had once asserted that the scheme of things
Was constant in its bargain with the earth,
Now advertised from every slope and hillside
A new exclusion, worse than frosts of winter:
Tongued in the trees, writ in the running brooks,
The law of contract and of property.
The horror of their hunger, so reflected
Even by burnished mirrors of rich corn
Was what they fled from in dumb multitudes.

34.

When mothers in the dark courts off the Strand
Were grateful to their scarcely visible stars
They had a child to sell that some gent wanted;
And it became a public nuisance that
Whole herds escaped from sweat-shops filled Haymarket
And Regent Street right up to Oxford Circus;
When in the *haut monde*, in the highest, best
Circles of all it was well understood
That wives, the ones a man would think worth having
Were bought, then made, the bourgeois thought it shocking.
The writers re-invented virtue and
Wept at the loss of it by these fallen angels.
Prostitute was a word of feminine gender.
What they did in the world was not for money.

35.
Surprised to find Heine died at fifty-nine,
So brave a soldier lasting out that long.
With Byron the first of the open-necked shirt brigade,
Breast bared to bullets and a songster's throat.
A lawyer too and took the full degree,
Which does not mean that he knew any laws
Except the ones we all know, heart and home,
Inertia, conscience, two and two make four
And one are three, old self-hood working out
A destiny in conflict with much else,
And, in his case, consumption of the spine.
Of course his German Jewish friend would work
On the harsh laws of history, instruct
Heine, who once had heard Napoleon's drums.

36.
Those graves in Père Lachaise. We saw his too,
A humble soldier in the eternal war,
My felon friend and I, a lawyer, as
He later was to charge. Yes, guilty as …
We sat where Liberty spread her skirts on gravel,
The box smell stronger in the heat of France
Mingled with wine fumes as we toasted him,
A lawyer without law, a rebel tradesman.
The birds in the black cypress tree nearby
Sang doubtless of sweet liberty as once
They had in Wexford, in the song at least.
Heine was pensioned by the French, such freedom
From everything except the lower back
Consumption and the Jewish pull, ours Irish.

37.
These liberation soldiers, born too early,
And some, like poets after Pound, not learning
That things had changed, as Heine's friend insisted.
Liberty, like all goddesses, could vanish
When you got up too close. She was the rocks,
The mountains and the sea, she was the storm.
Still freedom, still, thy banner, torn but flying
Streams like a thundercloud against the wind.
She wasn't Austria, she wasn't priesthood,
In Shelley's case she wasn't marriage vows.
Odd, though she pre-supposed for most some money, they
Did not connect her absence with the absence
Of cash, which could abrogate priests, vows, archdukes.
Rich liberals in Florence with their wives.

38.
For some she was colours on the map, not fast.
While Garibaldi's rebels fought, Cavour
Took in what dirty linen was on offer.
Triumph of red meant that in the piazza
Liquid Italian flowed, the Hapsburg Duke
Fled baggageless, escorted by his Austrians,
A wheel gone spinning down the slope, the abyss.
Funds in the bank no doubt with the freemasons
Finding a new relationship with bankers too,
As well they might, who now ran the Departments,
Rich peasants renting, but, the olive ripe,
Would rob and squeeze mere labourers in a press.
Yes, liberty was great, except for those
Who needed her the most, poor absolutists.

39.
Hating the hill, the hollow and the stream,
Horizons that were given by the gods,
It was for end of Eden that he yearned.
Surrender to the natural was all
The village offered the divided, when
The girls lost innocence they were received
With eager moanings straight into the sweet
Circle of sense that animals shared too.
The little screams from down the river path
Echoed complicities in old wives' dreams.
They mumbled still of sin, but when he trembled
It was for something other than this joy,
A thought which merely followed the blood's curve,
As common springing as a wayside flower.

40.
All in the end were friends here, ruthless games
Ended with lovers proved their clemency.
The treacherous wrestlings in the orchard grass,
The thunder of the heavy days in May,
The ponderous couplings of the callous beasts
Bore smiling innocence like crops that were
Blessed by the parsons at the harvest home.
The dawn in dark that was the city's glow,
The shining surfaces of its alleyways
Beckoned to strange complicities beyond
These happy minglings of opponent loves.
His breath stopped for the imminence of a place
Where all of Eden's terms would be reversed,
Love, hate, pain, pleasure wear each other's face.

41.
Baudelaire was "out" in '48
When Buisson saw him at the barricades
With double-barrelled gun and cartridge belt,
Both looted from the gun-shop round the corner.
He was crying wildly, "Death to General Aupick",
But did not add he was the General's step-son.
Later in *My Heart Laid Bare* he listed
Iis motives as a revolutionary:
"The thirst for vengeance." Yes, we know that thirst.
"The natural pleasure taken in destruction."
We know that also, our own hearts laid bare.
And lastly a more subtle one perhaps.
"The intoxication brought about by reading."
Yes, revolution is a bookish pastime.

42.
He persuaded Champfleury to call their paper
"Le Salut Public". The name recalled
Deliberately the Committee of the Terror.
"The violent and abnormal had a deep
Attraction for him", someone else records.
Alas the normal soon came back again.
After the hot June days the barricades
Were swept away like remnants of a fête.
Order, as many called it, was restored.
Large numbers wanted peace. He too perhaps.
"The patron saint of rebels is old Nick";
And Revolution was "the antichrist".
"When I consent to be republican
I commit evil knowingly", he wrote.

43.
Yet he was there. He made the synthesis
Between the consciousness of one's own sins,
One's sweat of soul, one's dubious private motives
And the clear merits of the public cause,
Beckoning like a bath to cool and clean.
If only those whose motives were quite pure
And hearts quite free from hatred could cast stones
Or root up cobbles for a barricade
It would be a lonely business, revolution.
No-one suggests the cohorts of reaction
Should be so free from the original
Stain as the ones who want a different world.
Indeed their stock-in-trade is to know all
The twistings and deceits of greed and lust
And make good use of them in daily business.

44.
Only the working class might still be loved,
Who toiled and died of white lead poisoning,
Hating the rich consistently, like Christs,
For only they were somehow still above him,
Gave him example in their suffering,
Could even be his heroes. They were soldiers
In a holy war against the virtuous,
The moral order of the bourgeois world,
Whose basis, as he knew, was prostitution,
Pleasing alike to prostitute and client.
Their servitude alone was not self-chosen
With wiles and graces, vile hypocrisies,
If they did not exist, proud victims in their hovels,
He would be alone, like Satan, in denial.

45.

Amid the roar of iron-hooped wheels on cobbles,
The rush of narrow shoulders through those streets,
Where ghosts by day accosted passers by
And memories weighed heavier than stones;
Or at evening when sad whores and clients prowled
Seeking to sell revenge or buy it cheap,
There was no place at all for such as he.
At home where cat and mistress gazed in cold
Uncomprehending savagery at the coals;
In theatres where women's eyes reflected
The icy centre of the chandelier;
With spleen and glee contending in his heart
He would know the double exile: he from them
And they and he together from the Garden.

46.

At country girls who caught their breath in wonder
Along the boulevard the lights winked back.
She worried in the wash-house steam about
The skin that bared would one day please the wankers
And, given a bit of luck, a rich protector.
Lautrec apotheosised her, made her crudeness
Tawdry no longer through intensity
As, stony faced, she danced her sad defiance
Of propriety or modesty or that
Innate sense of a woman's place in things,
Shy, virgin, fearful and a man's invention
Which all had brought from villages to lose,
Which men destroy and recreate and hope
In pervert hearts will still be there to use.

47.
The laundry left at last, her red-armed comrades
Joking in the steam, her name in lights now,
La Goulue was a star for five good years,
But then began to drink. Though Lautrec came
And Oscar and the famous Feneon
To see her as a fairground novelty,
The face grew coarse, lost line as well as charm.
Her nerve ends screaming in the fat for drink
She shared a stinking cage with starving lions
And rolling like a mountain round the ring
Wrestled opponents of her own weak sex.
The bored crowd drifted by to find some other
Mockery of what womanhood had been
Once, back where they had come from and their mothers.

48.
Girls on the river, girls at Argenteuil,
Under the dappling trees in August light,
Skirts full and creamy like cloth waterfalls
Brushing the grass, each ankle an example
Of how athletic angels are, as eager
They stepped on land at one of Sunday's stages.
The light declined at last. The dance began
And music mingled with the wine in veins
Alive to summer and condemned to Monday.
Passion like night might follow light's decline
And be at odds with openness of glance,
Which should have lasted longer. We could ask
Was the whole day as easy as it seems,
Their comradeship unclouded like the moon?

II

49.
What was it like in the Garden? As naked as birch trees,
Their skin as native a sight as sheen of the river,
The curve of buttock but as the curve of bole,
No cloth occluding its shock or smooth synthetics,
To cling, suggest, to ruck and to reveal?
And psyches without disguise or covering either,
Everything natural, instinctive, happy,
No kinks, no hang-ups and no fetishes,
No thought thought daring, or no thought at all.
It may have been a munch, but Baudelaire
Would not have been at home there, nor, in truth,
Might you, o hypocrite lecteur, less hyp–
Ocrite perhaps, more hip than them,
Those clear-eyed innocents in unshadowed groves.

50.
And one presumes equality. Of course.
Which wouldn't be like Milton, that's for sure,
Since he's quite clear about the dominance.
"Not equal as their sex not equal seemed;
For contemplation he and valour formed,
For softness she and sweet attractive grace;
He for God only, she for God in him.
His fair large front and eye sublime declared
Absolute rule." It would not do today,
At least in theory, though old Adam might
Still get a bit of what he got, which was
"Subjection, but required with gentle sway,
And by her yielded, by him best received
Yielded, with coy submission, modest pride
And sweet, reluctant, amorous delay."

51.
One likes that second yielded: "by him best
Received/yielded." His weight in other words
Not thrown about, but still some let's pretend
She didn't want to ... what? Oh well, whatever.
A little later on we're told that they
Being spared – "eased" is in fact the word –
The putting off of clothes (and underclothes?)
"Those troublesome disguises which we wear"
(Sweet catches, strippings, stages and delays)
"Straight side by side were laid; nor turned, I ween,
Adam from his fair spouse, nor Eve the rites
Mysterious of connubial love refused."
Make what you like of that "mysterious".
And, since we're at it, of that "nor ... refused".

52.
But female sexuality is not
Somehow a thing that seems to trouble him
In spite of his three wives. The impression is
Of love and duty happily performed.
Blind he could never see the drawn-back lips,
The teeth tips bared in that sweet ecstasy,
So sweet for the beholder, holder too.
Yet if he loved their womanhood as well
As his own masculinity, or loved
A different image of himself as male,
He sought, no doubt in darkness, love perhaps,
Those shudderings and that fierce abandonment,
His keen ear heard those cries, which, puritans
Of their own pleasure though men are, redeem.

53.
May not of course have found them, like so many,
Even most perhaps, tale all too sad to tell
And told too often in the marriage bed.
De Sade knew all about the clitoris.
Freud didn't, not at least in 1912.
Ms Carter in "The Sadean Woman" says
The eighteenth century aristocrat
("Lecher" but I must keep my iambic beat)
"Knew that manipulation of the clitoris
Was the unique (sic) key to the female orgasm ...
That this grand simplicity was all there was
To the business." Sade could learn.
Although a doctor the good bourgeois couldn't.
Knowledge is power, yes, but power is knowledge.

54.
But men they say had power, while women lay
In darkness through the ages. It's more likely,
Most thought it bully just to keep their nerve
And take their pleasure and be somewhat thankful,
Subjection but required with gentle sway,
Being, as Milton said, the best to aim at.
Of course most women were as ignorant
About themselves as any man could be
And so no tender whisperings at all
Could put things right, if any thought them wrong.
Millions believed that they were simply frigid.
Some thought that they were the odd woman out.
Lighten that darkness, Lord, let our time flower,
A rose whose opening is still full of wonder.

55.
Our fathers must have lain there in the darkness,
Candle ends guttering and the sweet dreams fled,
Imagining if that union could not be
That there could be no other in their garden.
Was it our fathers who lay there in darkness,
Watching the dawn come, dry-eyed now at last,
While marriage stretched before them like a life?
Or did our mothers all, like whores, pretend
Cheerfully sometimes, even, wretchedly
At others, or decide it did not matter?
Perhaps it was a class thing, as most may be.
You bought pretence or blithely did without it,
Secure in your own excellence and worth,
Or equally secure in ignorance.

56.
The early waves of western travellers
Caressed with envious eyes the glittering skins
Beneath the fern fronds, saw free-loving peoples
Made careless by ripe marrows of the morrow.
Paul Gauguin, burdened similarly with work
He didn't want to do, a wife who was
A complex history, longed like lecherous sailors
To share in such simplicities and be
A noble savage free of past and future.
It didn't quite work out. He brought with him
His absolutes and silly contradictions.
He sought the modern in the innocent,
Sought love with spirochetes in his blood,
Asked answers to the questions posed in Paris.

57.
The lower middle classes still believed
There never could be much and that much worked for.
And even the romantics were quite certain
That money could not buy the things that mattered:
The steady grey-eyed gaze of understanding,
Time waiting on a leaf in autumn woods,
The envied love of enviable women.
One hardly needs to add that they missed out on
Much that was merely a short drive away,
A passing taxi or a routine flight.
Journey they must if lovers will have meetings.
Nor do the happy ask when they have landed,
Why money like the ocean drowns all guilt,
Why the shore smiles on those who have attained it.

58.
It took five centuries to know for sure
That it was really so. The nobs adjusted,
Not without trauma, but as nobs will do;
And though we've heard about the *trahison*
Des clercs as if that sin was something new,
The fact is that the clerks knew all about
The sale of their poor goods a while before
The buyability of everything
Became accepted as a law of life.
(The author of the Rosetta Stone, a liar
Twice over, whether needfully or not,
Wrote, "Ptolemy, ever living, loved by Piah".)
No, it was common people who believed
The hierarchical lies which still remain.

59.
A handy weapon in the hands of those
Whose business was confusion. Finance now
In league with aristocracy, priesthood,
Conservativism of all kinds to pretend
The guiding principle of the world was not
How much it's worth, but whether it's worthwhile
And worthy and worth doing and of worth
In sight of man and god. Even Dickens's poor
Swallowed it with their gruel. Though the desperate
Might be benumbed past caring and the sly
Might have caught on quite quickly to the game
There were poor honest workmen in this century
Who suffered disillusionment as great
As first war soldiers finding their betters out.

60.
Quite common people, stubborn in their faith
As Kitchener's footsloggers, still believing
Long after it was known as lunacy
By all their lords and masters, that the world
Was by and large a place where one was called
To do some service, honourably and well.
The clerks – another sort of clerk –
In Pim's believed the ledgers could not lie:
You gave good value and the books would show it.
An eye for the fast buck and the quick kill,
The railroad millionaires, Jay Gould and Rockefeller,
Manipulating governments and trusts,
As foreign to their ethos if they knew
As later would be poor diseased Capone.

61.
City of dreams the tenors sang, the Danube,
Grey in the rain had veiled itself in blue.
The powerful were like children dressing up
In plumes and bear-skins, thigh high boots and breastplates,
Their children garbed like sailors come ashore.
It was the baroque, sustaining itself on disguise.
Even the buildings wore epaulettes like generals.
Of course what they wore off duty was formal also.
When hierarchs went out on the town to sample
The pleasures of the flesh they wore top hats
And opera cloaks with red or purple lining.
And in the novels and the melodramas
The toff could be a murderer or a king.
Only the poor were clearly seen as such.

62.
At the salon an over-dressed crowd saw Klimt had bared
One breast of an over-dressed model and found it shocking.
But the totally naked did not seem natural either.
The nudes of Egon Schiele were not rosy like Renoir's
Reclining, rejoicing in their own fleshly nature.
They were skinny children, stripped, at a disadvantage,
Sometimes resenting, challenging the gaze.
Karl Kraus said the Empire lived by the art of the drape.
The oppressor covers up and strips at will.
The victims loathe their own sad bodies most.
Of course there was Adolf Loos whose simple buildings
"Well-formed and comely in the nude", he said,
Would augur a new age of nakedness.
Still Schiele's girls sulk, are brassy or just sad.

63.
The body into which the soul was sent
Cringing from gaze, assessment, inquisition,
Had unclean parts and functions, shameful, nameless
Intensely conscious of itself but lacking
A happy sense of self as natural object,
Weaker than others, always vainly grasping,
Impotent as a jug of slopped out water,
Uncertain, imprecise in reach and compass
Recalcitrant alike to will and impulse,
A mere inadequate vehicle for wish,
Its many failures making imprecision
And approximation its habitual modes.
It was not the body's passions which dismayed
The soul but its unworthiness for love.

64.
These were the modern things. One spoke of Schoenberg,
Hoffmannsthal, Rilke, Kaiser, Stefan George.
The Secession was, as you might say, well-established.
One argued about Freud and knew that Mach
Had at last rid science of metaphysical ghosts.
It was really only ill-bred schoolmasters,
Post office clerks, Slavonic mysticists,
Those ill at ease in our great German culture
And politicians on the make who spoke
At boring length about what they would call
The problem of the nationalities.
And yet you know they made this jejune topic
Somehow the burning issue, though even the Marxists
Laughed at them. They did. They really did.

65.
With skill the slabs were blasted and then split
For billiard-table tops. The smooth slate sang
In harmony with the ivories, permanent, heavy
As rich Havana clinging to beige and curtains.
Now in the cavern which the quarrying left
Noticing the resemblance to a famous grotto
The parish priest has placed an electric virgin.
Six hundred yards from her the cable rose
Seaweed hung from the depths. Such hawsers bound
The new world to the old, Wall Street to waggish men
Bent over cues and cunts. A miracle
Is needed to restore the pristine wonders,
The stage-door Johnnies' joys, expanding markets,
The simple faith of villages and islands.

66.
In 1901 Marconi sent
Across the wastes a more ethereal message.
While Chesterton on the 9.15 regretted
Dying romance and blamed Lloyd George, the jews,
Moustaches tickled thighs as white as ivory
And gents and mashers hunted the same game.
The ether grew more bodeful, fleets assembled
Off stormy headlands hissed the stokers' fires.
The Boys Own Paper went to bed to taps.
Romance persisted, even on the Somme.
One morning as old Europe's sun brought dawn
A quarryman who was placing charges would
Look at the vibrant sky and see come in
A monoplane irradiate with rain.

67.
In Russia suffering is preached as a mode of salvation.
The poor are seen as martyrs, sometimes envied.
Mere endurance is sanctified by religion.
Our writing glorifies misunderstanding and pain.
Lenin rejected all this. I have never known
A human being so possessed by hatred
Of all forms of unhappiness and grief,
Suffering and want as he was. Yes, he had
A burning faith that none of them were essential
And unavoidable parts of human life
But abominations that we should regard as such
And could bring an end to. It was very striking
His vision of a snow bright, sunlit world,
Empty of ache, disappointment, hunger, sorrow.

68.
But even supposing that most formal crime
Was, as reformers said, a product of
Environment and sprouted from the dark
Sad walls of tenements or bred in parlours
With aspidistra plants; and further say
Our selfish and familiar agonies,
Ambition, envy, disappointed love,
Were gone like greed from human life somehow;
One wonders what of moral suffering,
The consciousness of wrong-doing, the ache
Of other lives in ours, of conscience like
A spectre with us in the noonday sun?
It's either that we'd do no wrong or be
Vultures in sunlight, picking the bone clean.

69.
Internalised self-punishment perhaps,
The super-ego battering on the head
Of the old harmless ego, just another
Of the notorious drawbacks we have bought
In swapping our old paradises of
The happy instincts, dancing on the beach,
After a day of murder and before
Some rough stuff fucking in the plaintain groves,
Whatever plaintains are, or mangrove swamps
Supposing you can fuck in mangrove swamps.
Yes, civilisation has its discontents,
But still there are objective wrongs, objective
Balances we're called upon to strike.
The rational vultures pick the eyes out first.

70.
Matisse had painted lovely nudes reclining
In joyous being, *Le Bonheur De Vivre.*
When he went to dinner with Miss Stein and Leo
He would see his rival's lyric painting there.
And of course he'd also seen the other one,
Luxe, Calme et Volupté, the centre piece
Of the autumn salon a few months before.
Comparisons with Ingres were freely made:
"A pagan joy". "The deep well spring of life".
He would paint some nudes. One night in Avinyo
A girl with heavy, sullen features squatting
Before a sailor with her cunt pulled wide,
Her back to us, beside her on the table
Another joyful fruit, a split, pink melon.

71.
The other demoiselles stand round about,
Accessible as melons on a table,
Their bodies savagely distorted, faces
Horribly expressionless, blank-eyed,
But posing in mechanic attitudes
Of provocation, joylessly assumed,
Routinely, to arouse mechanic lust.
The sailor is gone now, we are in the centre,
As brute as any mariner with money,
The squatting woman's head is twisted towards us,
A savage mask, dull, ochreous, diabolic.
"You paint as if you want us all to drink
Petrol and eat rope ends," Braque was to say
As penitential Spain proclaimed the modern.

72.
Marinetti went to see the guns.
Oiled steel recoiling. Plume. The answering puff
Among the crumbling terraces was death.
This was at Adrianople, 1912.
He had to prove a point, the only hygiene
Of the dirty world was war, and prove as well
That engines ran the show. Well, so they did.
With screaming gears the lorries brought the brave.
The Bulgars laid a railway down, the line
Blighting the orange groves. All except mules
And men was spherical, rectangular,
The ribbed skin of the flying machine composed
Of interpenetrating planes, its prop
A perfect arc. Severini would be pleased.

73.
"M. Bleriot has guided a plane in a given direction
Over the strip of sea that makes England an island
And under not too favourable conditions.
What the French aviator can do in 1909
A thousand aeroplanes can do in five years time.
When Farman flew a mile it was possible to say
An ingenious new toy had been invented.
A machine which can fly the channel is not a toy.
It is a deathly instrument of war."
The Times was wrong. The instruments of war
Are toys and toys remain till death do part.
With fixed guns firing through the Farman's blades
It was a schoolboy honour they redeemed,
Released into the infinite at last.

74.
In the summer twilight thousands filled the streets,
Embracing, weeping, eyes and faces shining.
And then as darkness fell there came the singing,
The old heart-breaking songs, the mighty, soaring
Es braust ein Ruf wie Donnerhall and after
The stern strong hymn of German Protestants,
Ein' feste Burg ist unser Gott. I moved
Slowly along the Wilhelmstrasse with them
It was as if I floated with the crowds,
Forgetful now of self, immersed like them
In a great tide of Germanness, of oneness.
Although what was to come was terrible
That night seems still august, magnificent.
I shiver when I think of it today.

75.
How sad the bugle in the wood's green depths
Aching for what is lost now to the world,
Least told of all tales now, least sung of songs
Since on those summer roads the marching boys
Sang out between the poplars in their dream
Of death in some great circumstance of friends,
Some proof of love beyond the dull demands
They never had expected, made each dawning
Among the little houses, little streets,
Between the window and the door of bedrooms,
In offices where courage was submission,
Where duty was a dragging chain and sacrifice
A grim sad burden carried to the end,
No bugle sounding, even for the brave.

76.
Hate was in short supply as were munitions,
And needed to be mass-produced like them.
"I hate not Germans," Edward Thomas wrote,
And he was typical in that of many.
Until Lord Northcliffe found the right imago.
Self-images were stronger. In imagination
A valorous self had waited which could be
Ardent, magnanimous and chivalrous,
Could prove itself at last a schoolboy's hero.
And it was strange how as the nations parted,
Their promontories reaching for each other,
Their shore lights vanishing beneath dark seas,
They were united in their knightly yearnings
As they had never been by saner visions.

77.
When I took the train my work was thoroughly abstract.
In the years before I had been, as I thought, liberated,
But at the front, without any break at all
I found myself among real, intractable things
And the men who worked with them every day of their lives.
My companions in the engineering corps
Were miners, drivers, workers in metal and wood.
On my first day there I was dazzled by the breech
Of a seventy-five, a gun which was standing uncovered
In the August sun, the magic of light on white metal.
This was enough to make me forget abstraction,
The art of nineteen twelve was dead for me.
Once I had fallen in love with that kind of reality
I was never again released from actual objects.

78.
In those first months of the war he grew quite thin.
The skull, which has always been near, showed clearly
    through.
Although at Cracow after Krasnin he
Had seen the stretchers jostled through the crowds,
The dead laid out in rows, the women wailing,
He never spoke of war as suffering.
He would open newspapers eagerly and read
As if he were burning a hole in every page.
The gruff good nature those who knew him best
Had noted as his mode of intercourse
Vanished. He was quite impersonal.
Worse, when he read of some atrocious happening
He would burst out laughing. His amusement then
Seemed genuinely uncontrollable.

79.
They showed him to the special waiting room
Formerly used by the imperial family.
The welcoming committee stood about.
He clutched a presentation bunch of roses,
Unhappily, not knowing where to put it.
Then Cheikidze made a formal speech.
"The principle task," he said, "is to defend
The revolution which has been accomplished
Against attacks from within and from without."
While he was speaking Lenin looked around,
Examining the ceiling and the walls
As though the sentiments he heard expressed
Did not concern him personally at all,
As though they welcomed someone else, not him.

80.
Then he stepped forward, putting down his roses
And taking off his bowler hat. Ignoring
The people in the waiting room he spoke
Through the open door to the murmuring crowd beyond.
"The peoples' need is peace and land and bread.
They give you hunger, war and landlordism.
The revolution has been just begun.
It must end in total victory or perish.
You are the advance guard of that victory.
Long live the world revolution just begun."
The committee was clearly uneasy at these words
But the soldiers now were presenting arms and the cheering
Was swelling under the roof of the station outside
To a great roar of joy and recognition.

81.
There were no lights outside except the searchlights
Which the Kronstadt sailors had brought from the Peter Paul.
These picked out the lettering, gold on big red banners.
The bands had begun to play the Marseillaise.
They carried Ilyich to an armoured car.
He stood on the bonnet and spoke, repeating simply
What he'd already said to the crowd inside.
"This is the world revolution just begun."
The cars then started for the Ksheninskaya.
Our headlights were the only ones full on.
In the beams we could see the guard of workers and soldiers
Stretching ahead on both sides of the road.
Those who have not lived through revolution
Can not imagine its great and solemn beauty.

82.
The time was ripe. At least they thought it was.
For the double helices of Tatlin's tower,
The dialectic process soaring upwards
In interlocking spirals, leaps and bounds.
In revolutions and catastrophes;
And ripe too for Lissitzky's Lenin tribune,
The leader over voids on leaning steel;
The Pravda building's bold transparency
Abolishing the concept of the wall;
The Workers' Palace with its outside girders,
Naked tension cables, ventilators,
Bridge and mass, riding on transience.
Whether the time was ripe or not it never
Will seem so in quite that way ever now.

83.
For these remained mere projects. Trotsky said,
"I know that meetings need arenas but
These need not take the form of cylinders
And the cylinders need certainly not revolve."
Lenin disliked most things that end in 'ism
And did not see how they were all connected.
The Dadaists in Zurich called themselves
"Conductors and condensers of the new",
The metaphor did not appeal although
Electrification plus the Soviets
Was now his definition of what next.
Stalin put gothic pinnacles on skyscrapers.
Sixty years later the Centre Pompidou
Proclaims the ripeness of another time.

84.
"The Council of Peoples Commissars resolves
That the monuments erected by the Tsars
Which have no historical or artistic value
Be removed at once from the streets and squares of our cities.
It is further instructed to mobilise the artists
To create maquettes of monuments which might
Be put in place of these abominations."
Erase the past, said Marinetti too.
"Museums are cemeteries where old corpses rot
In hateful rows. Though one might like to make
An annual pilgrimage on All Souls's Day,
One should beware the poisons one might breathe."
Pious commissars would have demurred.
They were concerned about artistic values.

85.
Although such forms astounded by their beauty,
Machines were innocent of beauty's claims.
Their mundane purposes had freed them from
The tyranny of ideal loveliness.
No fog of memory, remorse, regret
Clung to their clean, inhospitable surface;
And so men weakened by their women, mothers,
Priests and philosophers, ideals, honour,
Saw in their pounding shafts, their piston blows
Bright metaphors of what mankind could be
Freed from the mists and moonlight of the past.
Their metal hearts beat purposefully on,
Needing no visions, pledges, pacts with time.
For they were time and future, and time's pledge.

86.
Picabia at the wheel of a Bugatti,
The horn bulb to his painterly right hand,
Peaked cap reversed like any Kerry hurler.
Strange opposites, but both sufficing myths.
And this was better than the Kerry hurlers,
A strapped-down bonnet and the dream of booting
Round Brooklands or along the Great North Road.
The lower middle class did not believe
There could be women like the mistresses
Who kept him in such cars though he ditched both.
And ditched poor modernism too, to make a trio.
A member of the lower middle class
Might want a car, a wife but thought that either
Could only be afforded by the careful.

87.
There is an ignition lever on the wheel.
Advance. Retard. It could be also French.
Some did not know what frenching was of course,
But grew up playing games about ignition
While modernism passed its palmy days.
The dreams somehow were limited by boyhood
With no belief in possibility
Outside of the romantic's boyish head.
It would be traitorous to attempt translation
Into the real world: the ocean flyer
Never becoming pilot; the general, soldier;
Explorer, traveller; even the great lover
Being slow to learn the rudiments of love.
But still the advance guard held exposed positions.

88.
Girls achieved total being all at once,
Pressing on air like buds or bowls or fruit,
Curved entities which cup what they contain,
Not angular and pointed like the male;
Were intimate with air as blossoms are,
Disturbed, at rest, or crowding here and there
In sudden multitudinous response
To some invisible command or current,
Yet in still self-containment melon-like,
Secreting sweetness, one with their own substance.
To be touched. Not to be. Like all perfection,
Reproach, remembrance of another state.
Seeming like dream things, yet more real than he,
The opposite. The other. Yet quintessence.

89.

The blonde chicks in the movies knew the answers,
Moved their behinds ironically, chewed
Gum as the fellow talked, to his discomfort.
With cardboard shoes, two pairs of knickers and
Oddly enough not much that she could sell
In little old New York in twenty-nine
A girl had to watch her chances all the time.
Alone in the big city where the lights
Threw lurid messages of profit on
The bedroom wall, they learned the truth, but fast.
You gotta make a buck. You're on your own now.
I'm sorry baby, but it ain't for free.
Some affectations of sophistication.
Steam heat the air of freedom. Leaking shoes.

90.

Romantic Ireland dead as the man said,
If ever it was otherwise, its fated
Mother loving heroes mouthing clichés
Before a yawn, a dirty joke, a scuffle,
Their lives, their martyrdoms, moved Brother Welsh
To brave deeds with the leather every day.
Their purity, their shining well-scrubbed thoughts.
Made them remote as Íosagán or Patrick,
No real possibilities destroyed
Since death was all they asked for, the rope's jerk
Giving a first erection as a last.
We did not even see them as romantic,
The life they wanted grey as the grey schoolyard,
With grey beyond, grey houses and grey clouds.

91.
"The Biggest Show On Earth, A Warner Brothers
Vitaphone Production, Gold Diggers
Of Nineteen Thirty Eight", the net effect
Of those net stockings, forested in rows
Debated and deplored, a blow to morals.
Whether we were, as Father Fahy said,
Small victims of a Jewish plot to make
Satan triumphant, showing us such leg,
Or beneficiaries beyond old dreams,
A trick of light rays and of celluloid
Bringing that shine to eyes of village lads
Who never thought an eye would get that far
Wherever hands might travel in the dark,
Each kick a blow to something, if not morals.

92.
Let the city open tonight, an unfolding flower
Not yet full blown, glass petals tipped with promise,
Let it greet its lovers with wide embracing tracks,
Narrowing nearer to the nervous centre.
Let the neon signs throw roses on shining pavements
As the dusk of summer softens each separate vista.
Let the tigerish hide of the quarter proclaim a fierce
Energy in this decadence, this danger.
Let all be famous, but everyone to be anonymous,
Let all find their old friends, but stalk expectant
Through swathes of faces, seeking the lovely stranger.
Let the wicked streets be happy, the happy ones wicked,
Let us tremble, so great the depravity, lurid the darkness,
But come to the leafy gardens, finding the loved one.

93.
Let the city be spectacle, circus, arena this evening,
Its justification sensation, its poetry wonder.
And let it cling fast to its colours, unholy and gaudy
Forgetting the facts of its life, its grimness of purpose.
Let the news that is flashing through bulbs on facades be
   exciting
But innocent also. Let crowds in another city
Bring down a dictator, lone ocean flyers be sighted,
Sporting events bring riches to all the participants,
Records be broken in every sort of endeavour,
The roar of the crowd sustain the elation of sacrifice.
But over it all, like the neon red glow on the clouds,
The sense of a future the artists have comprehended
Demanded in manifestoes, foreshadowed in dramas,
Simple, electric and complex, achieved like the morning.

94.
This is a mother, not fatherland,
It nags its children, asking endless love,
Is helpless as a mother to provide,
And, sheltering them from the rough world beyond
Its curtains it unfits them for the streets
Where others are home. Her weapons are
Reproach, reminders of their lineage,
Their difference, the wrongs that have been done
To her and them, above all of the pain
That life has cost her and the sacrifice
She daily makes to fit them to undo
Such wrongs at last. No wonder that her children
Absorb it all as one confused long lesson.
She suffers for the sin of giving birth.

95.
We went to Brighton in our Little Nine,
The open touring model Leslie bought
On what was called H.P. A gorgeous day,
The sky was somehow deep, you know, like heaven,
I thought the bubbling tar might melt the tyres
And Leslie laughed, called me a silly juggins.
He was a lovely driver, doing forty
Once we were free of Staines. Its tommy rot
To tell us now that people weren't happy.
We had our own nice house, a tudor villa,
Which was the new thing then, a vacuum cleaner,
Dance music on the wireless, lovely murders.
Of course the war was still to come, that Hitler,
But it all seemed somehow new then, somehow modern.

96.
The trouble was that Busby Berkeley's girls,
Feet aching slinging hash or after twenty
Takes of the subway scene makes little difference,
Conflicted with a fiction still wrapped up
And packaged like the romaunts of the roses
Once read in old Provence. A modest female
Who yielded only to a courtly male
And never showed a flesh-curve to a stranger.
Freud said you pitch it high and then it's low.
Debasement part of it, dichotomies,
Something born not of bodies but of minds
Returning there. Oh sure I gave him head.
She didn't know, though, what went on in his.

97.
And we have sat, intent, in scuffed red plush
In scented darkness, watching Gable go
While someone else stayed home, back at the ranch
Perhaps, or at the base, neat, zipped or starched,
But hot for his returning underneath.
So many ages lasted the male dream,
Coming to us in tattered form while war
Ripped skies apart and Papa Hem rejoiced.
The scripts all said the girls were sweet on Clark,
But whether for his martial prowess or
His moustache ... ? Know the heart of maid
We may not, but the heart of man we know,
Mankind that is, both sexes interlocked
In senile dreams and conflicts, both as one.

III

98.
Everyone believed the Commandant
Lived such a wonderful life. I had my cosy,
Clean, well-tended quarters where I could
Retire and be at peace with wife and children.
Her garden was a paradise of flowers.
The children could roam free, their every wish
Attended to. The prisoners who worked
In house and garden never tired of doing
Small kindnesses for both my wife and children.
What people did not know was how I worried
How when at night I stood beside the transports
Or at the crematorium or fire-pits
I thought at length about my family,
Fearing for them in the uncertain future.

99.
And then there was my work. My sense of duty
Has always made life much more difficult
For me than for my colleagues. I worked hard,
Perhaps too hard, at everything I did,
And when they offered me another post
Which meant promotion and which I accepted,
I was at first unhappy. My involvement
With all I did at Auschwitz was so great
That I could not at first detach myself.
What I regret most now though is that this
Exaggerated conscientiousness
Deprived me of much time I could have spent
With my dear wife and children and intruded
On happy evenings spent with them at home.

100.
In the foyer of the Royal Festival Hall,
Great sarcophagus of the forties hope
That wars are fought for art-styles, liberation,
The English in community at last,
The soldiers of the avant garde at home,
An uptight crowd sips its pre-ordered drinks.
Here and there sounds the proper loud haw haw
But most have accents pining on a leash,
Dying a lifetime death in snuffles, whines.
They come in business suits or smart black dresses,
Dating each other after work or sharing
An anniversary with someone's parents.
It is the interval. The chords will wake,
True and transcendent. Then they'll all go home.

101.
A low black storm cloud stains the sky towards Southwark,
The water darkens, pocks and seems to thicken.
The concrete of the Hayward Gallery
Darkens as well. Stains gain an inch or two.
The modern ages as it surely must.
The railway age still lives. It clanks and drags
Another lease of life from Charing Cross
Over the river into Waterloo,
But *modernismus* did not change the world.
And art alas does not explode our lives.
These blocks being what they seem encapsulate
Its shock and seal it off. Like large transformers
They feed out to suburbia a current
Sufficient for an ordered people's needs.

102.
A path was laid to the door of the officers' quarters
Of cinders cleared from the incinerators.
Why did they order this? Why wish to walk
On such black ash so often, be reminded
(Which no one wants) of the job in their spare time?
It was not an ideal material.
Ashes would cling to highly polished boots
And in wet weather need some scraping off.
Was it a symbol of their victory,
So that each exit and return was dancing?
Was it of humorous intent, a laddish joke?
Or was it merely an indifference,
Abysmal, mortal, deep within their being
And lurking in the arteries of our world?

103.
Though Reich had said the real one must come first,
One day we had a sexual revolution.
Newspapers dangled girls like carrot bunches
Before male wage slaves on their way to work.
While real girls with minis to their eyebrows
Still had mysterious babies to look after
And solipsists abounded in the bars,
Technology brought Tahiti to the suburbs.
In Switzerland gnomes counted pills and profits
And dropped Repression as a ruling principle,
Installing Emulation there instead.
This was accounted freedom, Banks invited
Customers to borrow to enjoy it,
And work a little harder to re-pay.

104.
The strip clubs did a roaring trade, well not
Exactly roaring, more a gasp for breath.
The pleasure the packed patrons knew when those
Red curtains rose and all strained glumly forward
Was not so much the happy product of
Permissiveness as early prudery,
Sweet culture shock sustained by inhibition,
For some depending on a thin illusion:
Of girls as modest as the girl next door
Suffering shame at such extreme exposure.
Skin's palled a bit since then. There's too much of it
And "showing pink" is the thing in such resorts.
For the time being. Coals to Newcastle.
Diminishing returns an iron law.

105.
Sweet culture shock, sustained throughout our time
In never ending variations on
That simple theme established long ago.
The modest maidens, manly boys abashed
By their own boldness on a forest path
Have something left to shed, but when it's gone,
The geese which were so rich, the scaly dragons
Considerately following at heel,
To prove the boys all men, the demons who
Ate crumbs from such high tables thankfully,
Will they be then succeeded by the devils
Of accidia and emptiness, chimeras
Prowling the concrete roadways of the suburbs
As far removed from instinct as from joy?

106.
For many then sweet shock was part of summer.
Her going down was really going down
Into breath-stopping depths, the sonar sounder
Tocking the heartbeats off. Hair trailing back
Soft, heavy as she went, she dived far, far
Beneath her sisters in their Sunday best.
Dear Father Baudelaire, you said that sex
Was nothing much without the sense of sin.
Without abandon, sense of desecration,
Freud said, debasement, which may be a sin.
O sinking girl, please don't go down too far.
Put on your skirt and blouse again on heights
From which the depths of such falls can be measured
And let us still feel that sweet shame for you.

107.
Who watch the children anxiously lest they
Through mere familiarity with flesh
And flesh curve, bronzed all over now,
Return to paradise, see eye to eye,
The blue to blue, the grey to grey or green,
Not knowing old concealments and kept straight
By early love flow; hypocrite, you think
The streets too much resemble that lost garden,
Tight denims everywhere and nipples showing.
Don't worry. There'll be barriers enough
Whatever about yours. In this permissive
Age I've seen them huddle by the gables
Of the two bedroom houses in Ringsend,
Wrapped in each other, cloth and winter wind.

108.
Besides, the two beside the river bank
Were parentless, the Doctor was not there
To wag his finger, speak of introjection,
"Parental prohibitions and commands ...
Behaviour patterns, good or ill, becoming
Without our conscious credence, observation
The voice of our own super ego, warning
Prohibiting, suppressing ..." And so forth.
Yes, it could take a long and weary time
Before we'd all be fit for a new Eden,
The neuroses of the mothers visited
On daughters, who in turn would pass them on.
In fact he's almost saying, sins of fathers,
Right back to Adam's, the original.

109.
Ms. Carter is good on class and on the fact
That privilege extends to sex as well,
Not just in terms of what is sold out straight,
Women or ceiling mirrors, water beds,
Hugh Hefner's forms of happiness or forms
Of cosmic fear, but also what you do
When the landlord's on the premises, at the door,
Both parties nerves all shot with work or worry,
You are living with your in-laws, on the sofa,
Or when the walls are thin, the kids awake.
And then there's what your culture thinks is proper,
Keeping the light on even, travelling,
Over those lovely undulances, making
An evening of love's by-ways, making friends.

110.
If once it was the union of two souls
Meeting like storm-blown altitudinous ghosts,
A meeting which, however passionate,
Whatever that word meant on such bleak heights,
Was a bit cloudy, in our time it's been
Two bodies plus two psyches fusing somehow,
Or two mute bodies, urgent, ardent, thoughtless,
Or even one psyche, fondling its obsessions,
Which were the question and the answer too:
The challenge which contained the secret password,
The dread place which, when entered, could be heaven,
The pain which could burn into ecstasy,
The interrogation which could free us from
The torture and might speak our truth at last.

111.
Although conservatives will argue it
– There are flat-earthers also, travelled men
Who have been around the world and still have doubts –
Will even claim from their experience
That the conjunction we all hoped for, that
Of course we've all had faked for us by times,
Is a quite real phenomenon and common
The evidence suggests it's like the Yeti.
Take comfort if you must from text-book stories
Of joys made possible by "grind of bone
On pubic bone" or "tug on lips of vulva"
That union is gone, what we might even call
The common or garden one, except in movies.
The question is, why was it so important?

112.
As in old Lawrence's once notorious book,
Vide pages one eight one and one eight two
Of the prosecuted Penguin, the bit which
Caused all the fuss in fateful nineteen sixty.
Describing how his heroine responded
Old Redbeard almost writes in iambics, such as
"A strange slow thrust of peace, far down inside her ..."
"And ever, at the quick of her, the depths ..."
"And closer plunged the palpable unknown
Till suddenly the quick of all her plasm ..."
"She knew herself", he tells us, "touched, the con–
summation was upon her. She was gone."
There are five "deepers". Depth charge stuff all right.
The swinging sixties came in with a bang.

113.
And prosecuting counsel asked the jury
If they would like their daughters, wives or servants
To read it if they left it lying round.
In nineteen sixty, year of great departures.
He should have said their wives or gamekeepers.
Perhaps we have progressed a little since
And also since he wrote about those women.
"That are the devil to bring off at all."
"The sort that's dead inside; but dead; and know it."
That won't come when you come "and bring themselves off",
Its pretty clear how when he speaks of "writhing".
And then the diatribe on lesbians.
"They're nearly all", he says. And he could kill them.
The obscenity was not what it was charged with.

114.
Well, let's be charitable, old D. H.
Was blundering about in '28,
A pioneer; and maybe too misled
By Frieda, for whatever selfless motive.
But what about the chaps who've written since,
The chaps, we won't say chauvinists, renowned
As much for their adventures as their art.
In their hip books the obliging girls beneath
Our hero twist like salmon in a weir
And ask for nothing but the mighty poke.
And since it's only recently they've written
Of other forms of consummation what
We have here is a really stunning question:
What happens to the half of modern fiction?

115.
They used to tell us one should go to war
To get to know some things and meet some people.
You form a false view from your ivory tower.
And there was once a school of novelists
Who said they had outfaced the snotty bull,
Been barkeeps, shipped as ordinary seamen,
Shot lions in brown Africa, backed winners,
Sleeping with many women as they went.
All this in aid of knowing things about
The argot, the emotions and the facts
And proving they were men, not just mere writers.
Strange that the lads with legends trailing tall
Should know so very little about sex:
Their beddings egotistic, like their wars.

116.
There was supposed to be a Stella Gardens sequence
To put Yeats and his tower in their place,
For, after all, a visitor I had
Opined our little quarter had been built
For the aristocracy of labour – dockers,
Violent and bitter men perhaps when drinking.
The master bedroom measured twelve by six,
The other, square but smaller had no window
Since someone built the kitchen up against it.
The loo was out of doors. I don't complain.
In fact the Stella poems, like extensions
Projected, never started for the want
Of money, time and energy, were meant
To celebrate, as he did, rootedness.

117.
Or anyway a roofing. 51
Stella Gardens, Dublin, was the first
House that I ever owned, almost the first
Object of any kind except for books
And once, a car, although I was a bit
Past what old Dante called the middle of
The path which is our life. Am past it still.
So here I settled down in seventy-two
With wife and children, Iseult seventeen
And Sarah almost eight. I managed two
And sometimes up to four effusions weekly,
Facing the bedroom wall, my papers strewn
Behind me on the bed. There were no stairs
Or battlements to pace upon in Stella.

118.
And yet I was embattled in the way
That most of those who are embattled are
In our society. I feared the post,
The admonition from the EBS
Which threatened to uproot me every month,
The ESB which threatened instant darkness,
The GPO which threatened severance.
Yeats said, describing some half mounted gent,
"A man so harried that he seemed to be
Not one, but all mankind's epitome."
Well even a free-lance's situation
Though scarcely known to sociologists
Can still be seen in terms of common struggle.
Or so at least I, right or wrong, determined.

119.
I joined the NUJ. I wrote long pieces
About the need of state support for artists,
Tried to define an order in which art
Might find itself the breath of common being.
Some well-known ghosts appeared reproachfully.
"That's phony, all that politics and stuff."
It wasn't, but I felt a traitor to
The long tradition of the man alone,
Deriding all sides, driven out by all,
To feast on his own heart in scorn and joy,
The central one, in Europe anyway
Since Baudelaire surveyed the damned in Paris,
And one which part of me would still respond to,
As to no other myth of sanctity.

120.
The docks were dying. In Stella some had taken
Three thousand quid redundancy, grim word
Grim prospect too, although they didn't know that.
They'd sling a hook no more, but stay in bed,
Drink pints and read the paper, have a bob
On something that Our Traveller Correspondent
Thought might oblige. (Of course it mostly didn't.)
Technology had freed them, so they thought,
The new container dock just down the river
Where ten unloaded tonnage that a hundred
Had fought to handle in the bad old days.
In fact inflation, poised to take off, took.
They were wiped out, their little lump made useless,
And left without work, money, peace of mind.

121.
Their hope was not in heavy hours down holds
Where flour dust choked you or on docksides where
The east wind up the river scorched the cable.
Their hope was pleasant idleness, not work.
A decent option if you'd worked and could
Feel that you'd done your bit and made provision,
Furnished the parlour, built a bathroom on,
Brought kids up who would not disgrace their mother.
Its not of course "authentic living" (to
Quote Heidegger) nor would it do for me
Who wanted idleness but work as well
Which gave life meaning, was its sweetest solace.
At least our interests did not conflict.
All I would do was add to what they wanted.

122.
I brought O'Flaherty to Fitzharris's,
An old *condottier*, he said, a killer.
He sat there, head a carved-out block, and talked
Unreconstructed rubbish by the yard:
The second Dempsey-Tunney fight, the time
That Michael Collins had some fellow shot.
They didn't know who he was, but later on
He passed a little into local legend,
The man who had done great things, some said for Ireland.
They walked him singing back to Mespil Road,
"I did it my way" passing Beggar's Bush.
It was not true of them, perhaps of him.
He'd had some sort of stab at it all the same,
As everyone should have, even workers, husbands.

123.
No wide-eyed women loving martial ardour,
The striped ski-slopes precluding the sublime,
Not even causes left or marching columns,
The bomb, the last machine, no myth of godship,
The gas works an industrial exhibit.
A time of lost poetic, me and you,
Red Mars, the moonshots, Marilyn Monroe.
So many poets unhappy in this time,
Sucking the childhood tap root, lovely life-juice,
Milk churns or tweed capped fathers at the mill,
Searching for fathers even further back,
In the long past, last storehouse of poetic,
The dolmen on the bare front of the hill,
The prehistoric haze, the low sun burning.

124.
Although no pastoral is possible:
No one can really say the dolts can teach us
To mend our ways or give obedience grace,
To be more faithful to the wives they fumbled
Or stiffen ourselves against the east wind cutting
Clichés to ribbons, crunching graveside gravel:
Out of the genes we still make something, though
We are alone here with the jets in fenland,
Grey sea receding towards the infinite,
An ancestor is much, a tribe is better:
We call on Anglo-Saxon, Celt, and Dane,
Whoever dug the ditch or hewed the roofbeams,
To give us somehow oneness with our wasteland,
Though not of course the sort their devils gave.

125.
At Robert Kennedy's funeral the female
Mourners wore mini skirts to the mid thigh.
They were in black of course, clothes *haute couture*,
And skirts were short in 1968.
Their lovely legs and sad expressions made
A deep impression on the viewers in
The Sunset Bar in Des Moines, Iowa.
We watched them travel up the escalators
As they arrived at Pennsylvania Station
And felt another surge of sympathy
As the long limo drew up at the steps
And Jackie carefully got out at last.
It isn't easy to get in or out
Of autos wearing skirts of extreme shortness.

126.
Elvis the liberated liberator
When he was liberated into fame
Gave nightly parties to attract the girls,
Who came in droves. He liked them young
And innocent-seeming as was plausible.
Those who had been before knew that the king
Would take his pick towards 2 a.m. or so,
When a specially lucky few were asked upstairs,
Told laughingly to strip down to their panties
(He had a preference for virgin white)
And wrestle with each other while he watched.
If afterwards they went to bed with him
They kept their panties on, those small white shields,
Though stained with semen shielding him from something.

127.
As a child, he said, he had seen two little girls
Tussling in some backyard, their knickers showing.
His liberation was a narrowing vista,
A moment and a gleam. He made home movies
Of hired girls, fighting, watched them on his own.
But, to be fair, he liked girls' company
And had his steadies even that he romped with
In almost film-script fashion: boy meets girl,
The music's new, it's still the same old dream
And love is still an all-American game.
He could not bear to watch the films he starred in
But had romantic yearnings all the same
And knew some sort of love and married twice.
Millions have longings they can never share.

128.
If he hadn't been liberated he'd have probably
Passed for quite normal, would in other times,
And must have tried to be with his two wives.
Far gone in drugs as he was and then also
Fixated on imagination's fix,
The chances are it wasn't a success.
The sixties have a lot to answer for.
The movies shocked his Memphis bully boys
When they discovered them, or so they said.
Their first arousings must have been much simpler
And Memphis does not know that every oddball
Is but an infant, doomed to a response.
The complex in a life would be beyond it,
Its decadences heavy macho stuff.

129.
That delicate first comer shall be king
Doubtless, the gazing infant never safe
From visions of thighs or stocking tops or bra straps,
The god descending on a beach, in boudoirs,
In the school playground or a circus tent,
In baths, the dentist's, sweet induction comes
Anyhow, anywhere, through any chance,
A cousin's shoulders in an aertex vest,
A blue-clad junction underneath a gym slip,
A bared knee genuflecting in the chapel,
Praise be he shoots his arrows everywhere,
In mother's bedroom, bless his little heart,
While the drums roll, the chorus wheels, or while
The home side snatches victory at hockey.

130.
And blessed are those to whom he brings obsessions
Accounted normal, manageable, sweet,
Unbiddable as honeysuckle scent,
But accepted in the joyous jumble sale
Where slips, straps, smalls and circumstance compose
A flood, a breaking foam in which to drown
And bare arms, insteps, breasts and backs assemble
A hierarchical heaven singing praise.
Less lucky those whose first stab is bizarre,
Like Rousseau when his lovely guardian beat him,
And doomed the doleful ones whose apparition
Comes tinged with agonies of other sorts,
Hatred of mother metamorphosed to love
Of scrambling girls, bared, hot, humiliated.

131.
O lady of the moon whose profiled face
Halts our walk homeward underneath the trees,
Shine on unblessedness your blessing now,
Wed our desire with our desire to please.
Lonely Actaeon saw your bared, pale flesh
Through celluloid of water, silver bright,
And stood prolonging this unholy joy
Feasting on nerve ends in the moon's limelight.
You turned your back, autogamous as he,
But knew him gazing still on that expanse,
Turning to stasis what should be a dance.
Turning to wrong and sulkiness what should
Have touched with joy that whole nocturnal wood.

132.
So you reversed the roles, you would hunt too
And not for satisfaction of the flesh
But rage of justice which you would endure
When in the thicket you would see him thrash,
Torn by those dogs, the fiercest time had reared,
Perfected in dissection of their game,
Actaeon suffered doubly, dog rends, mauls,
And also incremental wounds of shame.
But if you through the agency of dogs
Gained rapture of revenge and righteous pangs,
You learned that also near a nearer bone
There would be severings by the self-same fangs.
So now let hunters and their prey be one,
Be prey, be hunter and all preying done.

133.
And qua tu fait de ta jeunesse, my lad?
I sold a lot of it to a pension fund.
We all sell, every one of us, to buy.
It wasn't bad, the routine of the office,
The country girls across the corridor,
The week-end booze-up, sometimes a good bang.
He sells his brain-time, buys a new Toyota,
A house on mortgage and the company
Of bright-eyed children, a neurotic wife.
He sells some brawn-time for a feel of breasts,
The pints and fags, the outings with the lads.
She sells some handling, an insertion or
A reluctant suck without the rubber for
The well-being of the child that bastard left her.

134.
Dowson found harlots cheaper than hotels.
He might not now, they pay high rents as well.
And neither would he find appeasement knowing
The dear-bought freedoms of bohemia
Denied to the respectable: strange term
From days when Ormsby, Gore and Atkinson
Knew that in order to be duns, not debtors,
They had to keep the straight and narrow or
Go sneaking out at night like Jack the Ripper.
Nowadays money and a mohair suit
Confer more freedoms on them than he'd have.
Now while he'd pine they're sucked off every night
And much respected for it by their peers
Who can afford hotel and harlot too.

135.
And where the system functions as I should,
The competition being keen and sharp,
If Dowson had a buck or two at all,
Having knuckled down a bit, say one semester,
A novel, culture noddings on the telly,
Sometimes at least he'd find he could afford
The lesser forms of harlotry, though lesser
In fact so far out by our fathers' standards,
Or even by Symons's somewhat garish lights,
That dealing in eschatology, the end
Of lives, or just of eras, plus debasement
As he did, he might come to wonder were
The harlots who were offerings such delights
As eager for an ending as himself.

136.
If that famous curious visitor
From lifeless Mars were still to come to earth
He would report (although, agreed, he couldn't)
That the inhabitants of this crawling place
Were all obsessed with something they called "love".
This was a state of mind, he would conclude,
Whose consequences for the sufferer were
That happiness was now impossible
For him or her without the company
And constant sexual congress with the loved one.
Oddly they used the same word to describe
A feeling many thought it was their duty
To have towards others, family, friends or even
Their fellow humans, in the lump, at large;

137.
They like to hear, he'd say, fine songs about love.
You hear these songs at all hours issuing from
Their little radios everywhere you go.
In restaurants, bars, the laundromat, the brothel.
It seems to be the first kind that is sung of.
The wanting to be with and fuck another.
The second as I say is more a duty,
Grimly and sometimes sadly undertaken.
What's certain is that this strange love emotion
Forlorn, despairing though it sometimes may be.
It's all that's left to them of the sublime
And almost all that's left of their vast searching
For meaning or significance in their state.

138.
After the phone call which the chairman made
To his lordship, still abroad, the towers descended,
Sliced neatly at the base, becoming clouds.
The tramlines stretched unburnished in the sun
And father stayed at home to watch the telly,
Which could not fill the silence with its voices.
His skills, an entail, now of no more use.
England which they had gouged and torn and shafted
Rested from agony. Their poets had said
England was parkland, pitheads an offence.
Let it be parkland then, be pastoral,
Dollars and Deutschmarks grass their white-fenced paddocks,
Red steel-flakes rust like leaves into the rivers,
Great oaks return and Arden be again.

139.
The discovery was they did not need the mills,
Satanic, dark or otherwise. The mills,
If mills they were, could be in places
Where yellow men and women without unions
Worked happily in denims day and night
While dividends flowed in to keep the fenced-off
Acres as acres should be kept. The puzzle,
The only one remaining now, was people,
The football-loving people of the cities
Whose differences were bus-routes on a map,
The Pennine clefts, the cobbled valleys, endless
Brick-yellow streets, who had once been torn like turnips
Out of the clodded fields, their screams unheard
And strangely had some call on England still.

140.
The line might well be drawn through Shakespeare country.
North of the woods of Warwick once had grown
The webs of brick and girder, the black pall
Beneath which a fair-minded people dreamed
Of self-help, co-operation, brotherhood,
While in the grimy mansions perched on hills
The pith was put in maxims: thou gets nowt
For nowt and little enough for tuppence hereabouts.
South of the line was lackey country where
Dickens's clerks had their descendants in
Computer people, form-fillers and chaps
Whose heaven still was hierarchical.
Well, some barbed wire and dogs and stiff policing
Would see the real England still prevail.

141.
On either side the river laps at smooth
And sterile surfaces, no wharves or pier stakes
Interrupt its fast sequestered flow.
A veil of moving traffic separates
Its dark expanse from Fleet Street and the Strand;
The artery is now where, rubber black,
The safe road takes the many home tonight,
Each Sunday traveller or family
Encapsulated from the world outside.
As dusk falls and the headlights show the rain
The scene seems curious, empty, silent too,
Although the traffic's whine is ceaseless and
Car radios interpolate the cries
Of love with bulletins of war and crime.

142.
On the Embankment side the Thames police
Still have a station, though their tin-roofed shed
Seems permanently empty, locked and shuttered.
Corpses, it seems, are rare. Most throw themselves
In front of tube trains now. In Dickens's time
Watermen trafficked in each tide's sad freight,
Along the Strand an elbowing gaslit crowd
Knew the cold water's nearness, sensed its threat,
And east of here, where homes were haunts and dens,
The middle class imagined mystery
And violence to be modes of life for millions.
Our terrors are both less and more immediate
Than when, quick, fecund, crowded, strangely homelike
The river sucked much closer to the heart.

143.
Sweating Bacardi over a tanned wanton
Who didn't want such baths, his lordship worried
About the electric fence, which didn't seem to
React to niggers somehow. As for dogs,
Those Dobermans were if anything more friendly
To stinking bucks than whites. Could they distinguish?
In fact, now that he came to think of it,
The only thing round here that had strong feelings
About colour was this whore beneath his belly,
Who arched and purred and eyed them at prick level.
He thought of England, green and cool and safe,
Of gravelled drives where no black maniacs walked,
Of servants bred from servants, then of dole queues
Composed of blacks and slackers. Such great problems.

144.
Off boulevards which flame in blue and red,
Like brimstone, where the serried coaches come,
Holiday-coloured, orange, pink and yellow,
Discharging senior citizens to enjoy
At a place Lautrec and La Goulue when eager
Had made a legend in another time,
Some hours of sanitised and distant strip,
Down darker streets are found by the more daring
Privileges which were once a great lord's prize,
The faces cold or pert, some beautiful
And not much marked by this impersonal traffic,
Many which, given other circumstance
To gaze on the high cheek and hollow eyes
Might haunt a true romantic all his days.

145.
The wheat grew thick beside the Roman way,
The curved stalks single, thick impasto strokes.
American grain killed off the market for it,
As, in the eighties, Engels said it would
So now it's pear trees, chemically boosted,
But you still see on the road to the Camargue,
Those yellow cornfields under that blue sky.
He went there in October, so did we.
They were burning stubble, making strips of black,
The flame first poppies, then the short stalks gone.
He never found the calm love of creation
For its own blessed sake, even in this south.
Under those burning suns, intensity
As much his theme as high recessive blue.

146.
In Saintes-Maries the Super Etendards
Banged through the sonic barrier, themselves
Almost invisible, tipped vapour trails.
He thought the peasant girls here beautiful
And painted boats, hauled up on the beach shingle.
There are no boats or peasant girls today
Except for pleasure craft, perhaps the blonde
Who pulled beer for the German and his dog.
Its bars and bungalows, apartment blocks
Around a tatty beach. October weather
Like a great shimmering gong, sea dirty bronze.
It's not much as a place of pilgrimage.
The Germans don't come here because of him.
The mutable, the modern now triumphant.

147.
And Arthur Scargill in his madness said,
"I see Jehovah in the wintry sun
Which looks to her like any golden guinea.
I see the lamb of god in England's fields."
And so on a bright day in England's winter
When Trafalgar Square lies dry and sharp and shadowed
We ask the right to work, close punk rock ranks
Beneath the heavy portico behind
Which shelter many splendid works of art
And underneath Lord Nelson who broke rules
But saved the bacon of the ruling class.
More moral than those rulers we reject
A life of idleness, a lack of aim,
Of purpose, effort, patriotic zeal.

148.
The right to work. Assorted publicists
And politicians who, quite rightly too,
Have no desire to work at any task
Other than those for which they feel they have
An unmistakable vocation, ask
On our behalf the right to other work
And so they might, for it's been bred into
The bent and grimy bone, this need to work.
It may be it will cure itself in time,
It may be we will learn to laugh and laze,
Our limbs stretched in the sun like animals,
To hunger, sleep and feed and know not it.
Meanwhile we see the dark satanic mills
Recede like visions of Jerusalem.

149.
Max Eastman wrote of meeting them on trains
When under Lenin's leadership the country
Was just emerging from the Civil War.
Middle-aged men with philosophic foreheads,
Motherly, grey-haired women with calm eyes,
A younger woman, sensuous, beautiful.
Who bore herself as if she had once walked
Up to a cannon's mouth. You would enquire,
He said, and you would find these were the veterans,
Taught in infancy to love mankind,
Master themselves, be free from sentiment,
The high traditions of the terrorist movement.
They had learned in youth a new mode from the party,
To think in practical terms, was how he put it.

150.
At a Party Conference in Moscow Province
A vote of thanks to Stalin was proposed.
Everyone stood and, smiling, clapped and cheered
Quite normally. But this time no one stopped.
No one would risk the dreaded accusation
That they were less admiring than their neighbour.
So it went on and on, a marathon
Display of stamina until at length
Some of the veterans collapsed, exhausted.
These were the veterans Eastman had described
A few short years before, a noble order.
Vowed like a knightly band to heroism
But with their patents of nobility
Not in the past, but in our human future.

151.
Our human future was to be quite other
Than that they had imagined in those years,
Waiting at tram stops in the freezing snow,
Keeping their assignations in the café
With newcomers who brought the news from Russia,
Living in libraries under shaded lights.
We know their future now (we know ours too):
Red star unblinking, sleepless, enigmatic.
Red sun which rose each morning over Moscow:
All seeing, like the God they had forgotten,
All knowing, in whose radiance their courage
Melted like dirty, wet, bedraggled snow,
Human reduction to the dirt on which
Historic boot-heels hastened history's end.

152.
Childe Roland to the dark tower came and climbed
The massive steps in natural trepidation.
But when the blonde beyond the blinding fountain
Asked him his name and business, his composure
Returned. He coolly showed his new ID
And obeying bored directions took the bronze
Lift to the fourteenth floor as he'd been told.
He smiled quite naturally at them while he noted
That Evil preferred its girls gaunt, doe-eyed, starving,
And thought it would be nice to get to know
The ones he met, while being quite aware
The person they responded to could never
Be himself. In the Dark Tower all tried
To be as was expected, not themselves.

153.
So he must change, invent and synthesise,
Suppress both cynic and idealist,
And hide as well the hate that filled his days,
Which fed his hope and love and tenderness.
He could use some of what he was, with skill
Deploying only aspects of the self.
Quite possibly the anarchist, the dreamer,
Used strictly for effect, with guarded tongue,
Might easily impress, beguile or charm,
As had the 'characters' in his former life.
But, after all, what is the self? The much
Discussed, mulled over, moralised about,
True self, was even perhaps mythical,
Was, anyway, a burden from the past.

154.
The first surprise was their delight in order,
Clipping and filing, typing, entering.
As if great things depended on exactness
In every single action. The new world
The Dark Tower was creating was destructive,
Oblivious, wasteful, with no end in view
Save further barren prodigality.
Within was category, calm and care,
The men in agonies of detail, logic,
Foresaw eventualities of every sort;
The slender fingers of the half-starved girls
Worked on with cool precision, almost gentle.
The end, in short, was stark and utter madness.
But the means used considerate and sane.

155.
And then one day his work was noticed, he
Was taken down the corridor and through
A padded door, to lunch with Evil in
An inner sanctum. And of course he loved it.
The subtle ambience of power obeyed
In silent smoothness and complicity
Is almost an aesthetic satisfaction.
But also there was something which to most
Of those he knew outside the building's precincts
Would come as a surprise. These men did not
Exude ambition, lust for aggrandisement
Like millionaires – or gangsters – in old movies.
Their gravity, their calm, their humour even,
Spoke only of the burdens that they bore.

156.
How many marches on Trafalgar Square
Since John Burns and Ben Tillett strode with beards
Nailed to their chins and Yeats' young friend stood guard
On documents which could hang William Morris?
The pigeons yield it up again. They know
The scrape and rattle of applause in tannoys,
Like pebbles being sucked beneath a wave,
Is not for ever. Tourists will return
Red buses and an active boredom reign.
If Neil Kinnock should go mad and maybe
Pull down the pillars of the gallery,
Proclaim the revolution, would we follow?
Another march ends now. The fringes drift
With furled up banners towards the nearest Watneys.

157.
And bloody right as that American
Said, "Its no job for white men going down
A mineshaft in a cage and digging coal
While the brief sun shines on a winter morn
And your lungs gather silicon dioxide,
Not any more, not in this day and age."
Nor any man, nor ever, since it can
Be done mechanically, even done without,
Or if you could get married on their dole
And bring up kids, keep pigeons, punt a bit,
Race whippets, do those other cliché things
That miners are supposed to do, or better
If days brought lovely purpose, clear and sweet
Extensions of each human faculty.

158.
Nor ever wonder if you were scrim-shanking
While others did the work, were just a scrounger,
Nor wonder either what it was supposed
To be about, this weary sort of life,
Nor sweat sometimes at night for fear that they
Would take away your dole or make it smaller,
Now that you'd lost all clout and couldn't even
Withdraw your labour from them any more.
But these are just day dreams. Their doles are not
Sufficient to keep racing pigeons on,
Have a few pints and punt a bit as well,
Hire video and films, buy tapes and records,
Support the heavy hours of idleness
Support life without purpose or achievement.

159.
When Patrick Kavanagh's mother took him to
The circus which had come to Inniskeen,
They saw among the other acts a man
Lifting enormous weights and staggering
Bow-legged around the ring, his biceps, eyeballs,
Bulging with fearful effort. After that
He lay down on a bed of pointed nails.
Attendants placed a plank across his chest.
Ten bashful local louts were then invited
To stand across it, their combined weight being
About a half a ton. The poet observed
It seemed a hard way for a man to earn
His living; but his mother said it was
Better than working anyway, she thought.

160.
"Bring me my bow of burning gold," they sing,
Linked hand in hand on the Labour Conference platform,
Their faces grey after a week of murdering
Tormenting words through composite resolutions
And phrases chosen for inclusiveness.
"Bring me my arrows of desire." They look
Like their desires, unacted, nursed
Through nights of envy, bonhomie and booze,
The pristine vision dying among details.
Outside is England on an autumn evening,
Skinheads and space-invaders on the front,
The televisions blueing the bow windows.
"I will not cease from mental strife" acquits
His verses of a mere utopian wish.

161.
And here where Evil was supposed to rule
He even found a sort of fellow spirit,
Of all the most remarkable, whose gaze,
Contemplative, amused, but not unkind,
Rested on Roland while the new recruit
Outlined a project with fresh eagerness
Or offered findings with due diffidence.
The intelligent are always lonely, always
In search of fellows; but intelligence
In enterprise at least is not displayed
In inquisition of the heart or conscience
As in the cafés where the jealous poets,
Debarred from action, enviously dissected
Emotions, motives, purities of purpose.

162.
His new friend spoke of the philosophy
– Or rather lack of it – the Dark Tower brought
To its activities. Alone among
The other power-systems on this planet
It was not tempted into ever seeking
To state or to define its ontogenesis.
Why should it bother? It did not appeal
To the Great Dead or seek a mandate from
The ancestors. It had no philosophic
Purpose that could be named, did not pretend
Or claim its power served any Absolute
Or Moral Order in the Universe.
The Dark Tower knew the philosophic vacuum
In which mankind now lived and welcomed it.

163.
Unlike the politicians on the podia
Who talked and tried to act as if they were
Able to adumbrate a common purpose
Transcending circumstance and even time,
Or the archaic power-systems still
Slowly decaying or collapsing round it.
The Tower did its work without pretence
To knowledge of man's ultimate destiny;
But was, he emphasised with almost passion,
The most important agent yet of history.
All others sought to limit and define:
The Tower alone to find and satisfy
Man's existential nature through his needs
And wishes, fantasies, hopes and desires.

164.

And what more noble end could be than this one?
Or what more democratic than response
To every wish, expressed through mechanisms,
Invisible, infallible, unerring,
Machinery so natural that its working
Seemed but a law of nature liberated.
It fought no wars; it summoned to no flags.
Its power did not depend on sad prescription,
On moral exhortation, old deceits.
It used its influence only to ensure
The neutral freedom which was necessary
To let it do its work, entice mankind
To enter on its future, realise
Without hypocrisy its actual nature.

165.

When Roland woke at night now in his new
White decorated, minimalist pad
From which all evidences of a soul
Thrashing around amongst its discontents,
Passing enthusiasms, short-lived fits of purpose,
All the disorder of unordered life
Lived in the hope of love and revelation,
Had been removed, replaced by the quite simple
Serenity of a resolved equation,
He heard above the murmur of the traffic,
Going about his business in the darkness
A voice ask what it profited to save
One's solipsistic, self-regarding soul
If one should lose the real world in that saving?

166.
Now for the first time in his life he was
Able to see the visible result
Of mental effort, speculative thought,
Theory and calculation. Once his joy
Had been in fitting thought to loving thought,
Premise to logical conclusion in
An ecstasy of clear contingency,
Now he was like an engineer who sees
The long curved line which was mere concept still,
Become a bridge tectonic, actual,
Hold fast and bear its calculated weight.
The metaphors his world had used for thought –
Foundation, edifice, conclusion even –
Now seemed to him mere childishness, pretence.

167.
The speaker is smart. No doubt at all of that.
His glasses glint. His punch lines are quite punchy,
And smart or not his heart's in the right place,
Which is to say, exactly where ours is.
Then why this vague unease one knows so well?
When the unanimous resolutions start
And everybody bleeds for the good cause
Why is one guilty, with them or against?
I listened at the NUJ, the protests,
Apartheid, Solidarity, the lot.
They applauded, right on cue, with righteous faces,
And laughed, with righteous glee, at easy sallies.
Why does being right seem wrong? I wondered,
Or protest seem so like complacency?

168.
No enemies, not even the milk-drinking
Fifteenth floor ghosts with six-inch fingernails
Who summoned starlets to share death with them,
Such ownership become invisible,
And moral like ourselves. Just like our own
Its grave deferral to the facts and figures
Appearing on innumerable screens,
Unalterable, though we peer again.
It has no separate nature, good or bad.
We share its greeds, its lapses, love of children.
Even its thin benevolence is ours.
Yet it commands earth; sickens crops
Blights forests; poisons oceans; hangs, a cloud
Of grim foreboding over river valleys.

169.
But gives life too, inspires the dance performed
By almost everyone. Scarcely an action done
But to placate this power, by day and night.
All the great rushing life of cities in its service,
The crowds on the long silent escalators,
The tangled traffic in the street outside,
The courteous workers, filing, copying,
The managers who speak into recorders.
All listen for its promises, commands,
Little is done without its sly approval,
Little for god, of course, but equally
Little to celebrate our mere existence.
Even when we pause, to dream or to create.
It measures out our moments like a meter.

170.
And philosophic hate the holiest,
Think of the brevity of this our state
The scope and eagerness of the human mind,
The sense of possibility we're born with,
Then of the lives maimed even while the child
Creates its first imagos, even in
The bed of sad conception, wondrous souls
Reduced already to a wretchedness
The animals would pity if they knew.
Most of life dull acceptance or pretence
Drudgeries for no clear end or reason,
For mere perpetuation of our kind,
Commerce, convention, avarice and power
Conspiring to construct the traps we're caught in.

171.
The wants he satisfied with his new-found wealth
Were strangely theoretical, as are the wants
The rest of us are told we have. He bought
What young executives are supposed to buy,
An Audi V8 4.2 whose engine
Was capable of greater speeds than ever
Could be attained on any actual road,
Gadgets which he never had occasion
To use or which were quickly superseded
By different models; cameras, recorders:
Ways to reproduce the images
Of places he had no wish to revisit
And never called to mind, aids which destroy
True evocation, memory, the past.

172.
Of course he had affairs. With gaunt, hard girls
Not unlike those he'd seen on the first day,
But more ambitious, possibly more able.
Nor were they like the girls he'd known before
In many sad cafés. These girls were not
The aimless waifs of that now lost existence.
They shared the Tower's *weltanschauung*, its values,
And though he didn't know that for some time
The Tower's ability to diminish, empty
And etiolate the sense of what was possible.
Even in bed, engaging in the acts
The magazines permitted, which were many,
There was this ebb of possibility,
This strange foreclosure of the human bounds.

173.
"I must do a starry night with cypresses."
Beside the clothes line where we hung the washing
Out at night to catch the morning sun
The cypress grove grew black against the blue black,
The stars beyond it splintered and enlarged.
(Myopia makes the stars more starry still.)
His moral suffering was very great.
Mine too, but his was madness, beyond cause.
In fact one finds it hard to comprehend.
His letters are no help, religious horror
Is not the same as moral self-reproach.
The modern has betrayed us as the mad
Him. We are still bound to the moral law,
Nor Vincent nor Gauguin excuses us.

174.
An asile is a refuge, the sad name
Suggests the mad have more to fear from us
Than we from them. We saw the patients walk
In shambling line as I had seen them once
In Enniscorthy, County Wexford, walk
The grounds of the asylum by the river.
Terrified, hoping none could climb the wall.
Although I know a little better now
In rational terms at least, I still hung back
Till they had vanished through the studded door
Which opens off the cloister before going
To have a look at Zadkine's sculpture of him.
I wondered what the patients thought of it,
A hero of their kind, and of our world.

175.
The Dark Tower stood, the tallest of the tall,
But strangely light and immaterial,
Its surface chaste, sheer, almost featureless,
A shining object, its reflecting glass
Making it sphinx-like, answering no question.
Acquisitiveness and greed proclaimed at last
As ruling principles of mankind's being,
Without decree, alike without concern
For past of future, or eternity.
The Tower decided for humanity,
Whether some ate or starved, what crops they grew,
Whether they lived in tents of sacking by
Streams thick with sewage fringing smoky cities
Or scratched the soil in gangs on mountain slopes.

176.
Roland delighted in its outward beauty;
Its chisel-thin, cloud-piercing, neutral form,
Unmoving against flowing fields of sky,
Now seemed to him Platonic, universal.
And also loved its inward-looking order,
The murmur of its air ducts soothing, steadying
Its calm and rational process of decision.
But it had roots as well, which stretched far under
Continents, seas and cities, reaching, gripping,
Blind, hungry, pale and white-tipped tentacles.
Engorging, pulping as they grew and fattened,
Groping for profit in their sightless searching,
Grasping the crumbling substances around,
Sucking the sweet sustenance from earth.

177.
When he was better and the weather summer
He sat up in the meadow there and painted
The edge of the Alpilles, the hanging sun,
A cornfield in the foreground, hot, bright yellow.
There is a reaper in the field, no symbol,
Not the grim death that he had done before.
It's flooded with its light and brims like prayer,
Unlike the twisted olives in the garden,
Done in the cold before his madness lifted.
Though some would like to pray or like their work
To be a prayer or an affirmation,
Lacking his madness, we lack his belief,
The agony of the olives, the corn's bounty,
Both alien to us in our sterile world.

178.
Quite shocking visions of despair and horror
Expend themselves against our calm approval,
The modulated space of boardrooms, bedrooms.
Are dealt in blandly by sophisticates
Who know the price and the occluding jargon.
Nor are "our merchant classes" philistines.
By their remote command a clean, lit place
White, windowless, unshadowed, limbo-like
Accommodates an endless series
Of masterpieces taken out of time.
A passionless acceptance reigns within
These air-conditioned spaces which absorb
To the faint murmur of a distant duct
The last assault waves of the avant garde.

179.
Ask not what end, inquiring traveller,
Is served, what grim need to placate a god
Or worship him, what visions, definitions of
Our destiny, our purpose threw up these
Audacious towers to shine in evening light.
The sun, a crucible of nuclear rage,
Knows nothing of such ends: it thrummed out rays
Of heat until the ooze transformed itself.
Money's convulsions too are life-giving,
Neutral, imply no purpose in our hearts,
But blaze upon this rock to make Manhattan
Rise in resplendence, such a culmination
Of history seen at sunset from the harbour,
Meaningless, astonishing and simple.

NOTES TO *THE END OF THE MODERN WORLD*

The following places and people, sometimes speaking directly, have not been identified in the text.

61-62, 64. Vienna.
66. Valentia Island, Co. Kerry.
67. Maxim Gorky.
70-71. Pablo Picasso.
74. Berlin, 2 August 1914. Friedrich Meinecke.
77. Ferdinand Léger.
78. Nadezhda Krupskaya on Lenin.
79-81. Nikolay Sukhanov and Krupskaya.
98-99. Rudolf Hoess, Commandant of Auschwitz. Almost verbatim.
108. Sigmund Freud.
145-146, 173-174, 177. Vincent van Gogh.

STRANGE

To have been born in the middle ages, a time
When berries were important, shining red,
Presaging apples in the bright hard winters,
When horses leaned into the frozen hills,
Straining against the faintly jingling harness, but
Planting their hairy feet delicately on the frost;
When gold leaf, thinner than snowflakes,
Gleamed on the cupola in the side chapel
And the virgin took the voices and the candle flames
Like threads into her slender, toilless palms;
When adolescent girls, aching with purity and aspiration
Vanished into the convent's bare, dismaying other-world,
Smelling of beeswax, without a backward glance
And the room in which a smiling devil had shown his cloven
    hoof
To the ruined card players just as the cock crew
Was bricked up and found to exist
Only by counting from outside the blank, staring windows;
When the earth was a floor, heaven above a blue ceiling
And hell a fire burning not far beneath;
When murder filled whole localities with dread,
Rumour like a foul smell spreading from town to town
While shopkeepers selling the products of the world
From wooden chests, open sacks and salt barrels,
Made the sign of the cross in acknowledgment of evil;
When the Latin vocabulary, so suited to prayer,
Supplication, adoration, devotion, benediction,
To iniquity, repentance, amendment, reparation and
    atonement
Ensured that the soul could be cleansed and re-born at will;
When all things stretched back to God
Like an aqueduct disappearing across the homely valleys:
To have been born then is to have been brought
A willing captive, in the train of some great event
Into another world, to be stood in its cities,
Agape and gaped at, ignorant of the obvious,
Confused between the longing for a different air
And the luck of seeing this garish wonderland
Awaiting a different salvation.

AGNOSTIC'S PRAYER

Our First Cause, who art most unlikely to be in any sort of a
location or habitation, heavenly or otherwise,

Hallowed be thy name, if you want it hallowed, and if you
have any name,

Let thy will be done, or, in other words, thy final design be
accomplished, unless it involves, as of course it might, the
complete extinction of ourselves and our universe,

And if, as seems improbable, you do influence events on this
planet, please give us each day, or at least each month or
each quarter, the necessities of life, including among
necessities of course the mortgage and hire purchase
repayments, the insurance premiums, the school fees and,
where applicable, the alimony;

Forgive us our debts to the extent that we forgive our debtors
and our trespasses as we forgive those who trespass against
us, while allowing for the fact that it is often not in our
power to forgive business debts, or trespasses once the law
has been invoked;

And lead us not into temptation, that is into situations in
which wrongdoing seems attractive to us, though in order to
avoid it we would also need to know what was wrong and
what was not wrong, which in many cases is very difficult
for us;

But deliver us from evil, if there is any evil in the cosmos
apart from the evil that is in ourselves, from which deliver
us indeed,

For, if we had any evidence of your existence and your
purposes, and if we could believe that those purposes bore
any relation to our ideas of the good,

How gladly would we say,

Thine should be the kingdom,

And the power,

And the glory,

For ever and ever,

Amen.

REMINDER

The brain is protected by fragile shields a fraction of an inch
  thick,
The frontal, parietal and occipital bones,
Easily shattered, cracked or penetrated
By bullets, flying fragments, sticks, batons and heavy stones.

And if those eggshell shields of the skull are broken,
Because you are a target or happen, when the thing explodes,
  to be walking by,
In a casual second all that you are has vanished,
Your brain and the rest of you die.

Nothing then left where once was all in all,
Those delicate cells and fibrils now gone dead,
The lovely leaps of current and connection over
By which we hold a universe in the head.

We did not grow great scarps, the foreheads of mammoths.
But erect and lithe, with proportionate head and face,
Depended on comity, compact each with the other,
From the moment one gripped a stone in some grey place;

And of course on imagination, reminding us that the other
Is also a consciousness, centre of cosmos and time.
Which weapons and blows can blot out: this tender reminder
Bringing home to our shrinking selves the finality of the
  crime.

1989

Imperial rhetoric adapted once
To comrades of the street or bed:
Tell them in England if they ask
What happened to your wits instead:
The two fires dust and damp ash, dead.

Nor banners elbowing as once along
The Ramblas like a river flow,
A transformation scene of wrong.
We see the puppet master smile
Hearing that open-throated song.

Analysis and learning led
To action which was always wrong.
No lodestar burning lone or high
Can show where faith has not misplaced.
The left is everywhere disgraced.

Nor logic, love, nor bombs, nor fire,
Nor in that island of the west
Returns along the bloody gyre,
Desperate expressions of the letch
For the lost land of heart's desire

Will give us any other than
The state we're in. An honest man,
The noblest work of God, admits
That whether they were low or high
Those poor old dreams have lived their span.

The night shift with their sandwich tins,
Their faces lined and tired and grey,
At the last tram stop by the trees,
Dream also in this cloudy May
Of flats and cars and better pay.

So let it go then like a time
When beauty or a silly dream,
Groundless of possibility,
Lit up your days. Since what may seem

Selfless is often self-esteem;
And vanities the preacher said
Are at the root; since hindsight shows
The usual psychic masquerade;
Does that mean we must let things slide,
Trust, like Lord Russell, to Free Trade

While millions die of interest rates
In Paraguay and Bangladesh;
The last brown trout turns belly up,
And acid, sent by corporate fates
Falls like soft dew on all twelve states;

And suffer the great spirit dearth,
The pointless agonies of birth
Whose issue is inanities,
Since no-one now will ever see
The kingdom he proclaimed on earth?

ATHENE'S SHIELD

On Athene's magic shield the wars which toss
   islands about and throw
Mountains into the air are followed by
The Peace of Ceasar. Beaten into bronze
The very vocables in which
The captive nations sing their glad acceptance.
Caesar seated at
Apollo's snow-white threshold dreamed his dream.
Snow-dazzled, blinded by the Alpine sun,
He sat too long,
As Charlemagne or Barbarossa in
The magic mountain, petrified at last.
Then woke to worse than what the shield had told:
Waste and division, hatreds, wars and chaos.

Within the shield, shield beaters,
Who make a breathing likeness out of bronze,
Sculptors who coax girls' glances from chill marble,
The measurers of all things, large and small,
From unimaginable stellar space,
To the invisible power packed in substance,
Great Vulcan's engineers, who toss bolts skyward,
Making long curves which leave a bridge behind,
The trades which turn the earth to teeming pasture,
Tilth and vineyard, meadow, orchard, grange,
Logicians and philosophers, constructing
A moral order, intricate as music,
Poised over chasms, echoing in space.

And lastly law-makers, who graft tradition
On to the tall growths of our errant wish,
Transliterate the alphabet of dream
Into the adult language of our will,
These on the shield as well,
Within the Aegis,
Bequeathed from the first
Enunciations of our human state,
Native to rivers, mountains, fields and woods,
The loved geography that bounds the dream,
But godlike too in possibility,

And never so much as now, when, suddenly,
Europe unfolding like a flower fulfils
Itself in new forms, new integrities.

POEM WHICH ACCOMPANIED THE PLANTING OF A TREE OF LIBERTY ON VINEGAR HILL, 14 JULY 1989

Far from the eaves and spires of brilliant Paris,
Unpinioned now, part eagle and part dove,
In strengthening circles soared the miraculous bird.
And everywhere the people raised their eyes
To widening skies where soon the bird might be.
Those bowed and bent in labour
Watched for its shadow on the waving corn,
Spoke in the patois of the poor of hopes
Cherished, unrealised through mastered ages
But fiercely lived through now in every parish.
Over the bright May meadows soared the bird
High in the Wexford sky; the baronies
Of Forth and Bargy, Shelbourne, Shelmalier,
Saw it enhaloed for a moment, lost it
In all the welter of hot history's day,
The dire confusions of the actual.
On Vinegar Hill above the pleasant Slaney
A tree is planted now to which the bird
Dovelike descends. O bird of freedom rest
Forever on our hills, our parishes,
Let Liberty for which all pay such price
Be native to our fields as those of France
And all the lands where men and women wait
An end of servitude see brightening skies,
See circles widen where the bird may come
For whom our world is insufficient home.

ADMIRABLE

Yes, but it still seems to me admirable
That Miss Weaver should have written
Her letter to *The Times*.
It had appeared the morning of the day I went to tea with her –
Cucumber sandwiches, cut thin as English
Courtesy sometimes is
But hers was not. She called him Mr. Joyce.
I had wept in the pub in Wembley the night before
As the television showed the tanks pushing
  barricades aside,
Returning to Budapest. Now, she said, in effect,
The tongs poised and her keen eyes questioning my response,
Was the time for all good women
To come to the aid of the Party:
An old red, with the good manners of the good,
And a place in the hearts of the civilised forever,
Defending what no liberal could defend
And no right-thinking person, then or ever.

SHADOWS

The old cars in the old movies were real, the box-shaped
  sedans
And the roadsters with white canvas hoods
Pprring along dusty roads, passing out streetcars,
Speeding down real streets, past real people,
With the spare wheel strapped on at the back,
Celluloid sidescreens and a tool box on the running board.
The old cars in the new movies are mostly mockups,
Fakes on new frames, even though they go pprr pprr
And have wirespoked wheels and vertical windscreens,
Bulb horns or horns that go gooa gooa.
But the old cars in the old movies do not exist any more.
They are only shadows now, a trick of light.
Whereas the old cars mocked up for the new movies really
  exist
And are kept in garages to be used again.

SORRY

Yeats,
I'm sorry.
I took time off to mend Sarah's skates.
A heck of a job. I couldn't get them right.
The time that should have been given to breaking up iambics
Was spent in trying to get them tight
Enough so that she, not me, could take flight
Of a sort. And I only have a few hours a week
Free from hack
Work in which the heart could speak
If the heart knew how to write
The proper kind of verse.
And then when I thought I had them right she came back.
I had made a hames of it.
Even after I did them all over again
They were actually worse.
My screwing and unscrewing were in vain.
The way it is now Sarah has no skates
And I have no verse.
I'm really sorry, Yeats.

ENCOUNTER

When I was looking for a place to kip
In a bombed-out house
Which smelled of fog and burnt wood
Just above Lord's cricket ground
One night in the late forties,
On the landing where the stairs turned
I almost stepped on an old woman.
There was a fierce practicality about her going.
Gathering her bundle,
Rushing past me into the fog.
She had made a sort of nest for herself
Out of old newspapers.
There was no use calling her back.
She knew what men were like.

RELATIONSHIPS

A bore at a party
Can accelerate the ageing process
In the skin around the eyes.
The plain girl with glasses in the corner
That nobody else is talking to
Can make you feel very small,
Morally and intellectually,
By her response,
Or nonresponse,
To your illconsidered,
Kindly meant,
Rubbish.

Many a man would rather take his chance
With a Sherman tank in open country
That had a bit of shelter
Than with a wife alone of an evening,
The telly switched off.
Many a woman mysteriously
Unable to free herself
From that horrible thing, a husband,
Would rather serve out her life-sentence
In a well-run female gaol.
And children,
Opening to dream
With the vulnerability of flowers
Which curl at the edges when touched,
Find themselves bound,
By love, no less,
To parents they know to be
Stupid weaklings and cowards.

But then, put it the other way round,
Think of Crusoe's man, Friday,
Naked, smelly, ignorant and
Not a word of English.
What a blessing he was,
What a heaven-sent addition
To the scheme of things.
A friend in need is a friend indeed.

There are hundreds of girls,
Living in plywood boxes, called furnished rooms
In the streets around here,
The not very sophisticated products
Of Innchigeelagh, Kilmaganny, Stradone
And other centres of the universe,
Many of them praying for dates,

But almost any one of them could be the answer
To the central problem of existence
If she came into someone's life
When he had nobody else to comfort him,
Or play games with him,
Or reflect him,
And at least one out of three of them,
Well, say one out of five,
Could stop Don Juan dead in his tracks
By just batting her eyelashes.

"All that's wrong with me is that I haven't enough
Money and can't find the right woman,"
Declared Kevin Sullivan.
Then he amended it.
"Any money. Any woman," he said.

There is enough in each of us to be the answer
To almost anybody's need,
Catherine's, Casanova's or Jesus Christ's.
Provided they were not distracted
By what seemed a more promising offer.

FUNERAL

The fourth this year which obligation or old affection
Impels me to, I kneel and stand,
My knee-caps hurting on the board
As when a child, noting who's here,
Who not, and singing dumb.
The homilies vary in their insult to
The horrid mystery, but most, like this, still make
A staggering presumption, our old pal
Is Somewhere now by Someone welcomed home.
Outside a chill east wind reminds us all
We too are frail and mortal.
Crabwise I edge towards a black-clad wife
And what may be his children, wondering what to say.
Then greeting old acquaintance tell a story
And get a slightly gratifying laugh.
It may be decent now to put one's cap on.
Yes. In the midst of death we are in life.

THE INTELLIGENT MR O'HARE

What a lot of stupid people my lot is cast among, said Mr
    O'Hare,
Looking at his colleagues in the office, having a few moments
    to spare.
They go on and on about the most abysmal things,
Golf, gardening, holidays, birthdays and engagement rings,
I don't know whether the women or the men are preoccupied
    with things the more trivial,
Though the women tend to talk about family stuff and the
    men about matters more convivial,
And my wife at home is scarcely a giant intellect either, he
    said, thinking of his wife at home in their house which stood
    in its little plot,
About whom once in the long ago, he had cherished the
    illusion that she had a good unformed mind, which he now
    knew she had not,
Though the way he put it to himself was that whatever mind
    she had is now totally destroyed
By the ridiculous obsessions and anxieties she seems unable to
    avoid.
I say ridiculous, he hastened mentally to intromit,
Not because I think Sinead's relationship with her boy-friend
    doesn't matter a bit,
Or that whether Aunt Julia leaves her any money or not is
    entirely a laughing matter,
It is merely that there is a difference between constructive
    discussion of these things and obsessional natter natter
And there is an absence of other kinds of interests in the case
    of my wife
Whose range is as narrow as that of a saw or a sharp pointed
    knife.
I do miss Joe O'Reilly since he went to Brussels he thought,
    not for the first time by any means,
For Joe read books and the heavier papers and the magazines
And watched the sort of television programme devoted to
    what is called current affairs,
His interest in that subject being really just as great as Mr
    O'Hare's,
Who could tell you what each dictator said he stood for in
    every part of every continent,
And what was his relationship, if any, with the Soviet Union

or the CIA and the State Department,
And who got his drama from the news which unfolded each
    night in cumulative ways,
Event unfailingly capping event before his astonished gaze,
Until the media lost interest in that particular altercation,
And the people of the countries concerned went back to their
    lives of more or less quiet desperation.
In fact it was mostly current affairs which concealed the void
    for Mr O'Hare,
As religion used to do for his father and mother who came
    from Clare,
As discussion of Ireland's chances in the World Cup did for
    the men of Mr O'Hare's floor,
Or as comparison of engagement rings did for the girls in the
    typing pool next door.
Unlike Mr O'Hare we should be tender to people's needs in
    this mater of concealing the void,
For it waits under our human feet, inapprehensible but
    thanatoid,
And we raise defences against it, knowing all the time that it
    is there.
Even if the defences we raise also convince us that we are
    better informed citizens, that we have a mind and that we
    use it, as they did for Mr O'Hare,
Concealing the void is in large part what we are doing
And also, paradoxically, passing the time in the most
    appropriate way possible, which is something we should
    bear in mind when we compare our own interests and
    activities with all the other interests or activities which we
    could be pursuing.

IN PRAISE OF HESTIA, GODDESS OF THE HEARTH FIRE

A goddess with no stories about her
Is obviously exceptional.
Though your average goddess may sometimes claim
She wants to be alone,
She hears the void hiss when she opens
A magazine which does not mention her name;
And nearly all are ready
To throw good men aside like sweetpapers
While risking everything except, they hope,
Their looks for a whirl with an oaf who will,
They secretly suspect,
Eventually sell the story to a tabloid newspaper.

How strange then that there should be one
Beautiful inhabitant of the divine village
Who is never involved
In a public brawl with another woman
Or a law suit with a former lover,
Who will never stage a hysterical scene
For the benefit of the bystanders
Or the gawking barmen;
And who, though the sister of Zeus,
Is neither a snob nor a dissatisfied intriguer.

And little wonder too that we turn
With relief and joy to the worship of one
To whom no stories attach:
Hestia, goddess of the ever-burning hearth fire,
Of the suspended coal.
In her dealings with mortals
There are no dramatic entrances and exits,
No stand up, knock down, drag out ructions,
The goddess appearing as whirling sword wielder,
Screaming blue murder and bloody revenge,
Nothing except the ongoing,
Almost untellable tale
Of human content,
Of love's flame enriched by its shadows,
Of how walls have stood while the wind of malice

Moaned like a lost soul without.
She is the protector of all who,
However foolish their once lives,
Come to her as suppliants.
Who demands nothing except that when we come

It is as individuals,
Not as members of a crowd or caucus,
And as ourselves,
Not as heroes or saints or statesmen or sages,
More like ourselves
Than we have ever dared to be otherwise,
More like ourselves
Than we could ever hope to be but in her presence.

AUBADE

The mess you are in is mostly of your making.
This is what waited, what you could not see,
Which thought of course occurs as dawn is breaking
And through the day will keep you company.

This is what waited, what you could not see,
Coming to mind as sequence, dialogue,
And through the day will keep you company,
Anticipating like a clever dog.

Coming to mind as sequence, dialogue.
Novels are lies which deal in resolution,
Anticipating, like a clever dog.
It may be there is simply no solution.

Novels are lies, which deal in resolution.
This is yours now of all those many lives.
It may be there is simply no solution.
The worst is what no enemy contrives.

This is yours now of all those many lives,
Which thought of course occurs as dawn is breaking.
The worst is what no enemy contrives.
The mess you are in is mostly of your making.

NO PROMISE

Nor were we promised
That the moon would shine again thus,
As it sailed through the narrows of the clouds,
Aurifying everything,
Tree-tops, roofs, gables.
And there was no undertaking
That the blue would again be that blue,
An indigo universe,
Deeply mysterious.
The moon is an ordinary moon,
A pale, dead reflector of the sun;
The night blue like the day blue
A mere effect of space.
What we saw was miraculous.

ON SEEING LORD TENNYSON'S
NIGHTCAP AT WESTPORT HOUSE

And did he suddenly, while the little train clunked over the
  long stretch of brown bog outside Castlebar,
The farewell gaze of the younger Miss Browne still warming
  the impressionable cockles of his poet's heart,
The memory of her ladyship snoring through *Maud* last night
  becoming at last less painful,
Or while it clacked pasts the undrained fields between
  Claremorris and Ballyhaunis –
"They really are a feckless people, they never do anything
  except out of immediate need" –
Or perhaps as the Gothic spire of Roscommon topped a tangle
  of untended trees –
"They live in hovels but they spend thousands on churches" –
Did he suddenly remember
That he had not put in
The blasted nightcap?
And, seeing in his mind's eye the offending garment lying
  huddled on the bedside chair,
Hearing in his mind's ear how he had said to Lord Altamont's
  man,
"I'll pack the overnight bag myself,"
And remembering how he had reminded himself, I must put
  that in,
Did he wonder in panic,
Would they send out for one from the Shelbourne?
Or would he have to go shopping in Dublin?
– An appalling prospect, not to be entertained.
But he could not, he positively could not be without one on
  that draughty boat.
He would get his end.
And so, as the Byzantine mass of Athlone Cathedral swung
  into the frame of the window,
Did he sit in gloom,
Becoming aware,
Once again,
Of
The heartache
At the heart of
Things?

WITHOUT US

1.

The vast and silent forest, I had read.
And it was vast, as day by day we learned,
But it was never silent. Working west
We heard it clatter, screech and sing from first light on
And even into night, but what was strange
Was that so little that it said seemed a result
Of our intrusion. Yes, a scurry,
A beat of tangled wings, a sudden squawking,
But then it would resume its endless talk,
Each creature to its kind, the noise of nature
Being, unbeing in a ceaseless shuttle,
The wind in the tree tops, growth and fall and death,
As if man hadn't, never would intrude.

2.

In all those miles of rolling prairie grassland
We never saw another human being. It was striking,
Each day's advance across the humming, stinging,
Thick, bead-headed grass. No savages,
A distant stretch of antelope or bison,
A sudden mist of birds, a lengthening snake,
Night creatures' burrows and their midnight pain;
And always through the day the piercing flies.
We knew that when we'd passed each new horizon
Our passage would be nothing. When the flies
Forgot our salt's intoxication they
Would feed, excrete and die just as before,
The grasses twitch, the bison nose on northward,
As if mankind had never been and nature
Had some mysterious life to live without it.

THOUGHTS ABOUT WOMEN'S BEAUTY

Beauty, said the old stories,
Brought a prince to the cottage door:
So you put your trust in princes.

Beauty, so lusted after,
May help you to get across the street
Even though the lights are changing.

Beauty of eye and feature
Can give you a false view
For a while of your wit and charm.

Beauty, unless saleable, can not be used to solve
The problems that wear it away.
It may even land you with some of them.

Beauty, supposedly valued,
Is common in the noisy dives
Where women sell themselves cheap.

Beauty, attracting poets, lechers,
The self-absorbed,
Seems too to attract the fates.

Beauty, a sad enough song
Often, for others, is a sad song enough
For some who are beautiful.

HOW THEY ARE ATTRACTED

How they are attracted
To the sadness of her thin, pale face,
How this evidence of a troubled childhood,
Making her timid before fate,
Enhances her beauty for them.
They are drawn to it like hunters.

OVID

Perhaps nobody much moved any longer by such a tale:
A girl running in maidenly fear,
The god pursuing in divine lechery,
She turning into a virginal tree;
But touched still today by the poet,
Telling a distant story, saying
"Her hair simply tied back by a single ribbon."

LIVING ON AN ISLAND

What happens here is more important than what happens
over there.
But what happens over there is more momentous.
What happens here often seems unreal.
But what happens over there does not really matter.
People here seem slightly daft.
But people over there seem deficient in understanding.
You can always escape from here to there.
You can always evade things there by coming back here.

You were born here.
You can be re-born there.
And again here.

On the night sea
And above the clouds
You realise that

Here or there

Though
Everything
After all
Is finite,

Nothing
After all

Is final

AN INTERRUPTION

We discern the dimmer peoples through the degree of their
apparent respect for death,
Having few other proofs that they ever existed save
The monuments, the food vessels or the weapons
They accorded their noble corpses for the long night of the
grave.

And so we think death bulked large
Over their active days,
Larger than harrow or harvest,
Larger than life and its praise.

We think they gave all their thought to the end,
The raising of the passage tomb,
The enactment of rites to dispel
The evil in its gloom.

We are wrong, probably. They probably gave little enough
thought to death
As they worried and toiled.
It was probably no more to them than it is to us,
Similarly embroiled,

So that when the great stones were raised only a few were
truly engaged
With the impenetrable mystery
And the rest with the settlement of a river valley
Or the pride of a dynasty.

Death may even have come as a sort of surprise to them, this
abstraction
Whose import they could not truly feel,
Until they began to gasp and choke
And found it was real;

As it certainly surprises people now,
For however it may arrive
It is always a sort of distressing interruption
Of the business of being alive,

Whether it comes gradually
After a long trial of nerve

Or pulling on the wheel in a horrified
Unavailing attempt to swerve.

Whether propped on the pillows,
Staring death in the face,
Or after enjoying a joke with the prettiest stewardess
Securely strapped in your place.

Even those who have had some warning continue
To plot and connive,
Repenting, disposing, worrying
About those who will still be alive,

As if something depended on the outcome,
With which they were personally concerned,
Or it was the living that had to be placated
And their approval earned.

And, yes, in a way it is nobler,
It is at least less craven, more like we are,
That we live so absorbed in time
In the light of a temporal star,

And by dint of absorption,
In a way transcend
The limits of our existence,
Its determined end,

While, in a place set apart,
With procession and ritual phrase,
We give death importance without letting it dominate
Our oblivious days.

THE NEED OF WORDS

Envy of painters:
A common writers' complaint,
The calm, unassertive
Statement of paint
Without self-revelation,
Claim to emotion,
Use of the word "I",
Only celebration,
The light touching the planes of the face,
The luminousness of the inner thigh.

But now through you I discover
That the painter's art,
However satisfying,
Would only in part
Suffice. It might convey
Beauty of body and stance,
Perhaps even love,
But how could a painting say,

That to you
And to your advent
Are due

Whatever of joy,
Whatever release,
Whatever accord;
Whatever of boy,
Whatever of ease,
Whatever reward,

Whatever of fate
Now half-understood,
The past
A wood
Through which I found you
As it was getting late

Accepted now
The measure of the dance
Half-heard

At last.

HAPPINESS

Sometimes, walking along Westland Row
Thinking that Anna will be there before him,
His happiness is so great,
He is like a walking jar,
Full to the very brim.
So full that it even spills,
Slopping a little over,
On to the pavement,
Into the gutter.
As he crosses over to Mr Sweeney's
A balancing act is needed.
In the shop he straightens up,
An amphora, a cistern,
Still swayed by the deep slop
Of happiness inside.
As he leaves the shop,
In spite of his best efforts
A little spills on the floor.
Mr Sweeney calls to his assistant
"Maybe you'd better get the mop."

SEX-WAR VETERAN

I've been a soldier in the sex-war for forty-something years,
Promoted once to corporal for mastering my fears,
They took my stripes away again for pitying the dears.

I've seen some hot engagements where much mercy wasn't
  showed,
Where chaps who took it hot and heavy paid back what was
  owed,
And I won't say I stuck fast to any gentlemanly code.

Yes, I've been in some tight corners and I've got some wounds
  to show.
I've soldiered under tropic moons where tropic breezes blow,
And had my balls near frozen too, in realms of ice and snow.

Oh yes, I've seen some funny things and have some tales to
  tell,
And I've learned some things you shouldn't learn, at least this
  side of hell –
But would I sign along again? The answer may be, well,

It surely wouldn't be the cause, which wasn't very plain,
Nor what came after victory in any one campaign,
When every ranker should be king, and setting up to reign –

We never won a spat like that, a clean-cut victory,
With native populations grovelling, down on bended knee.
It was ambushes and skirmishes and sometimes hard to see

Just what was peace and what was war, or who had won the
  fight
When at last you found a billet and you bunked up for the
  night
And the only transport sailing was a transport of delight –

It's more that for some kinds of bloke – and I think that's far
  more
Than have ever answered roll call on a palm-fringed heathen
  shore –
When they come to think back on it all and reckon up the
  score,

It'll be the thing could bring them near to some reality,
Some intensity and meaning in the blooming verb, to be,
That wasn't in the rest of things as far as they could see.

PITY THE POOR MOTHERS OF THIS SAD WORLD

Mothers have been having a hard time of it lately.
No wonder the greetings-card manufacturers have been
  spending millions to give motherhood a new image.
Those anxious little women who worked their fingers to the
  bone and stayed at home every evening praying for their
  children, loving them so much they got cancer,
Have of course long since vanished.
What a drag they must have been.
But even to be the object of any noticeable mother-love can be
  dangerous nowadays.
At best you are a closet homosexual. Everybody knows
  homosexuals have loving mothers.
You may even be some sort of a psychopath.
"His mother had a terrible time of it. But she lived for her
  children. And he was her favourite."
Hey. This guy is probably dangerous.
If there is a serial killer (of women) on the loose within two
  hundred miles (and when is there not?) the police
  immediately put him on the list of suspects.
When they pull him in they say, "Tell us about your mother,
  boy."
And every time you read a biography of one of the great
  dictators, a really formidable serial killer,
Some monster who wore jackboots in bed,
You watch for the mother factor.
Mostly you find they were devoted sons.
And in league with mother against some poor slob of a father.
While they waited for him to come home,
Usually so drunk he could hardly get his belt off to beat them,
They loved each other like turtle doves.
And when her son started his great purge,
Brooding and mooding so much that his wife left him,
His little old mother came and stayed with him
And sacked all his housekeepers
So that she could make his cabbage soup for him
The way he always liked it,
Long ago when they were happy together.

It used to be mothers-in-law that were the joke.
Now unfortunately it is mothers.

To have her mother ringing her up at the office all the time
Is an embarrassment for a girl. "It's your ma again."
But worse for a fellow. "Your mother has been on again. She
    would still like you to ring her."
You jerk. You mother-dominated wimp. You brute without
    feeling.
Yet what more natural than that a mother should be worried
    or depressed,
Or hitting the gin at home and desperate to talk?
Mothers soon become redundant now, like people in other
    jobs.
A mother in retirement used to be someone with neat grey
    hair and hands folded, waiting for her children and
    grandchildren to visit on a Sunday, glad to have a rest.
Now it is someone who is on the phone all the time,
Agitating herself,
Running up giant bills which her son will have to pay,
Suffering from withdrawal symptoms because worry about
    the children has become, like all worries, an addiction.
And the mothers who haven't got time on their hands never
    had any time anyway.
They were out all day like Dad and too tired and irritable at
    nights to tuck their darling up in bed,
Or listen to all that stuff about bullying.
Of course both the mother who is specially loving and the one
    who just shakes the cornflakes packet and runs
Are a recipe for disaster later on.
The psychologist wearily resigns herself to the certainty that
    this cripple had one or the other and that his wife is learning
    about it too, but fast.

Supposing one had a choice, though,
A mother who is too much there
Is perhaps the worst.
We all know about Proust
And how she only bent over him for a brief moment
In an aura of violets or something on her way to the ball,
Thus giving him his asthma and in the long run
Incapacitating him for anything except
The writing of masterpieces,
But the one thing everybody fears most
Is mother suffocation, to have your mother
Endlessly leaning over you

Stinking of some stuff made from orchids or the glands of
  little animals
Could result in far worse than asthma,
Or even an ambition to write novels.
Most men spend most of their early lives avoiding
Mother suffocation; and it is because of mother
That they first learn how to be
The experts in avoidance and concealment,
The cheats and liars and ingrates that they mostly are.

Heidegger says correctly that to be
Is to be guilty. He is wrong, though,
When he says we came from Nothing
And that this consciousness of arriving suddenly
Out of the *Nichtlichkeit*
Gave us the guilt.
We all come from a mother.
Everybody who ever lived had it all started off,
The anxiety, the decision-making,
The envy, the hopeless yearning
For someone to take care of us
By two other human beings,
But since paternity is, as James Joyce observed,
A highly theoretical matter,
It is mothers who get the blame.
So what chance really have mothers got?
The way things are now it is going to be hard
To persuade the greetings-card manufacturers
To keep this motherhood thing up.
After all, why pour any more
Good male money
Into an already
Lost cause?

THE MANIFESTATION

They did not fling themselves to the ground,
Tearing their anoraks,
Scrawbing their flesh with their nails.

Pulling up the sods,
Heaping clay on their heads,
Wailing ayee, ayee.

They stood there gawking,
Nudging, comparing, pointing.
And when afterwards they went

To the plywood lounge
With the persistent children
For Harp and red lemonades, sandwiches and tea,

They discussed what they saw or didn't see
Only with eager banality,
As they might a goal-kick or a glimpse of a celebrity.

Thus did they welcome
The goddess's manifestation, the vouchsafement,
The split in reality,

Driving home in the family car
With the persistent children,
Going to work the next morning

With a story to tell,
A five-minute focus of attention.
Since this was all, why

Why should the goddess
Ever deign to split
Our imprisoning reality again?

1798

Commissioned by Comoradh '99 and read on Vinegar Hill

They wore their Sunday best for early battle,
Coming with ribbons in their hats to join
Their neighbours at the crossroads by the chapel
As on a holy day of obligation.
War is release and sudden holiday,
For some, release now from a nightly horror,
The flaming thatch, the mingled oaths and screams.

The lovely summer weather gave them leave
To sleep beneath the bright and beckoning stars
And wake each day to Liberty's wide dawn.
But nothing happens as a wish would have it;
And war is chance, its currents rip us far
Beyond all headlands and all reach of rescue,
Beyond what heart can hope or soul can stomach.

Too soon the Slaney's waves were stained, the Barrow
Carried its cargo seawards from New Ross
To cold, wide waters where no sail appeared.
Their columns heaving now with frantic households,
Not heroes, merely people, but the pikes
Their hedge and shelter in the broken weather,
Here on this hill they stood, where we assemble,
A civic gathering in a different time.

History, the nightmare from which all mankind
Must struggle to awake, recedes at last;
And our normality accommodates
The dream of Liberty, Equality
For which they had to rend the normal day,
To take the lives of others, give their own;
Which seemed so distant then, to us mundane.
We should recall the price they had to pay.

THE LOVERS

I went for a walk one evening
Through the streets of the city wide.
There were couples laughing and talking
And kissing on every side;

And I knew that for some that evening
In the city's golden haze
Would glow as a remembrance
Through other, different days;

That some of them would be loving
Through times which would seem without end,
Passionate, gentle, caring,
Friend to sexual friend.

And I laughed with the happy couples,
Lost in a fond embrace,
Till I saw some in the future
Stand in another place,

Saw them glare at each other in anger
And rend each other with words
Like the claws of cruel leopards
Or the beaks of terrible birds;

Saw a time which would come for many
When, wounded and full of spite,
They would even rue the loving
Of this lovely city night.

And I prayed to Aphrodite,
That she might ease the pain
Which would flow from the bitter quarrels
Of parting, if parting came;

That the love which she now gave them
Might still somehow outlast
The lies and the resentments,
The twisting of the past;

And asked that she might spare them
As they tore themselves apart,
The fearful loss of fealty,
The freezing of the heart.

But as I walked up Dame Street
On my way home again,
I knew time holds us hostage
And that time brings us pain;

And thought at the chimes of Christ Church
Of the ever-flowing stream,
Bearing us into the future
As into another dream.

THE MINOTAUR

1.

On these hot midsummer nights
Under a white moon,
When the breeze is like breath on the face
In the old part of the town.
The listeners can hear
The thud of the Minotaur's hooves
Spreading under his weight
On the packed earth of his lair;
Can imagine the swinging head,
The thrusting shoulders, the red
Glare of his bulging eyes.
As ceaselessly up and down
In his awkward trotting he scuffs
The dust, then checks and turns
With a renewed surprise,
A repeated shock of rage
At the limits of his pen,
That small pre-destined space
In which his discontent,
His power, his possible grace,
His terrible yearning is caged.

2.

And at the end of a day
Of heat when the twilight comes
Bringing a vague unrest
To the girls and boys who stroll
Over the brow of the head
Where the eucalyptus trees
Catch the first faint stirrings, the turn
From a land to a seaward breeze,
Hinting of other places
And other half believed in
Possibilities,
We can hear his deep bull moan,
The almost heartbreaking sound
Of eternal isolation.
We know it too well, this note,
Of unending separation,
An unquenchable, deep, dire
Long agony of desire.
More, more, he seems to cry
A deep, reboant moan,
And then louder, lifting his head,
With a horrible, full bawl
And his bull mouth open, All,
As if by giving him More
As we have done, time and again,
Or even, All, All,
We could somehow end his pain.

3.
But we know it does not end.
When we usher those trembling girls
Whose budding, pulpar breasts
Under the ritual blouse
Seem eager to meet their fate,
Into the labyrinth,
We end his agony
Only for the curtate
And derisory duration
Of an evanescent span,
One short hour's ecstasy,
One achingly brief and passing
Night of debauchery.

4.

But so great his pre-occupation
With frail unlasting beauty,
His boundless, insatiable need
Of firm but tractile thigh,
Of malleable white belly,
Of brow and expressive eye,
His huge and ungulate greed,
That I have thought of him,
This stinking unwashed, gross
Shit and spunk-stained beast
Ravening to possess,
As another worshipper
Making endless oblation
Of beauty to itself.
And, as we brought from the boat
Each doomed consignment, thought
That in some new group might be one
Before whom as incarnation
Of beauty's very self
– That imperatorial power
Which all make oblation to,
The gods on their rocky thrones,
Mankind in the threatening world –
He would sink on his calloused knees;
That this unregenerate beast
Might confess himself pierced at last
By some quintessential girl
Who, standing there, lithe and alone
With bladed shoulder and bone
Might exercise dominion
Over his carnal strength
And gentle him forth from the dark
Shadows of his maze,
Black in the white moonlight,
Till he, like us, was free
In a world unshadowed, bright
With open pathways, fields
Where, garlanded and good,
Even he might sport and play
In innocent delight.

5.
They say that a hero will come
Some single-minded boy,
Who, having known only joy
And undivided love
In all his aspirant days
Will be totally unafraid
Of entering the maze
To which our thoughts return
With a horrified fascination
Nightly and even on days
Of calm bright sea and sun;
That this sunny-natured one
Will go down its narrow lanes
Black shadowed under the moon,
To find the ultimate den
In which, in cowardice now
Will lurk Pasiphae's awful son
And drawing his bright sword
Will kill the monster within.

6.
And I hear them also say
That this undaunted boy
With his open, smiling eyes
And the killing he will do
Through his passionate wish to destroy
The evil in our midst,
Will bring to birth at last
A new and better world,
Unsecretive, purged and clean,
Where all will have open hearts
And frankly smiling eyes;
Where, manifest, unafraid,
With nothing to hide or rue,
A proudly stepping beast,
Desire may go naked too;
In which never again will there be
Such places as our city
Here by its ageless sea,
Hides in its culpable
Secret complicity,
Labyrinthine, ancient, dark
Lairs of evil where
The anthropomorphic beast
Involves us all in bane,
Son of an ancient sin,
Fruit of an ancient shame.

7.
Tomorrow is the day
When the mighty goddess is carried
Around the bounds of our town
And its tunnelled, crumbling wall.
The young will sing and dance
Strewing flowers in her path
Alto and treble will rise
Towards a cloudless sky
In the ancient hymns of praise.
Then later the solemn dances
And the intricate choral songs
Will testify again
To what she gave our city
So that it lives in peace
Among its fruitful hills,
Descending terraces,
And twinkling olive trees,
The red earth newly turned.
And all the arts of accord,
Of co-operative endeavour,
Shipbuilding and architecture,
Calm counsel round the board,
Politics and law.
The goddess gave us all
Which a city may enjoy.

8.

But even the very gods,
Blessing and fructifying,
Warding off evil from all,
And keeping us safe from harm,
The living and the dying
In cot and palace and farm,
If the simple rites are observed
And obeisance duly made
By the rulers and the ruled,
As surely all must agree
They should be, even by us,
Enlightened and civic and free;
Even the gods we love
Can be suddenly, threatening, high
As the thundercloud which looms
Disastrously in the sky;
Are as often at wilful odds
With beneficent principle,
As the enemies of good
In human shape can be:
Insensate, deaf, unjust,
When moved by desire to possess,
By paranoiac rage
Or sportive wish to destroy;
Even perhaps by lust
For some slight human shape,
An uncaring girl or boy
Sighted one summer day
In the fields with companions
Lost in their day-long play;
Can relish our human pain
Or be merely oblivious
Of each terrible consequence,
Shrugging with cold disdain
When all are crushed beneath
The blindly turning wheels
Of indifferent circumstance;
Bringing war and famine
Plague and pestilence,
A terrible discordance:
Unstringing the instruments,
Confusing the orators,
Breaking into the dance.

9.
And he is of the gods:
His mother, Pasiphae, "she
Who shines", the lovely daughter
Of the life-giving god of light
Joy and illumination,
Helios, the one great, bright
Source of all clarity,
Tricked to a shameful, sordid
Untellable copulation
With a sottish, silent brute,
A beast of the weedy field,
By Poseidon, the sea god, whose
Shimmering, flashing domain
Of sun-blessed summer water
I see when I mount the steps
Up from my little house,
Stretched in its linear beauty
Under an azure sky,
Whispering of peace
But concealing in its heart
The whirlpool and the chasm,
The dark and dreaded abyss.
The storm so great and vast
It tears the world apart.
Born of such parentage,
He is both beast and god,
Disconsolate, stupid, slow,
But terrible in his turn
As his helpless victims know.

10.

But I hear them speak as well
On the pier wall, when the nets
Are stretched to dry on the bollards,
And in cafes during the pause
While the dominoes are gathered,
Of his endless ravening hate,
His cruel lust to destroy.
Yet when in bed in the hot
And sleepless nights they hear
His lascivious bull bellow
And imagine him stirring again
His bull flanks writhing once more
With unbearable desire
In the stinking dirt of his pen,
I know they turn to their women
With almost as fierce a lust
As taurine, dark and cruel
As indifferent to response.
Their need almost as his
For another so possessed
As to end its otherness
Its eternal separation,
To devour it once for all
In some terrible assertion
Of force and dominance,
One final subordination.
And they reach for a partner to find
In the yield and pulp of flesh
A brief cessation at least
Of the taunt that beauty offers
The torment that it causes
Merely by drawing breath
Into its cage of rib,
By its most artless stance,
Its endless, unintended
Erotic gesture and dance.

11.

We will all be as one tomorrow
In celebration of that
Which alone makes possible
The ordinary city,
Its life, its civic peace
Mundane normality,
The blessed agreed restraints,
The placing of holy bounds,
Awareness of others, pity,
The attempt to find some grounds
On which to base our claim
That rules and punishments
Are part of a greater good.
Sanctified and blessed
By custom, ritual,
Libation, sacrifice,
It will all be as it should.

12.
But then at some point in the day
The sun may chill, the sky
Darken, even its blue,
Become suddenly more metallic
Colder and further away,
When we hear across the roofs,
The angry, insistent roar
Of this unspeakable, huge
Leviathan of lust,
Rearing up again,
In gross, tumescent desire,
Ravening to extend
His merciless empire
Over another batch
Of chattering, bright-eyed girls,
Everyday beauties still
Ignorant of their fate
Whose pale, black-stockinged thighs
And behinds in swinging skirts
Might on another day
And in other circumstance
Turn the heads of men
In a boastful off-hand way,
But whose progress through the streets
When brought from the Athens boat
Brings hundreds out to stare,
And, alas for our human state
And its deep hypocrisies,
Many even to gloat.

13.
And many there in the crowd
And among the participants
In choral song and dance,
Even among the priests
Who will stand, white-vested, grave
At the temple to receive
The goddess home again,
When they hear the pain-pierced bellow
Of the beast who is kept apart
Will know they are hearing an echo
Of something in all being
And deep in the human heart,
Something caged and hidden,
Which no hero can ever root out,
However bloodied his sword,
And no new order suppress;
Shut, raging to be supreme
Which, sleepless, stirs unbidden
In the familiar prison,
Of our morality:
The thicket of deceit,
The woven, thorny, maze
The labyrinth of lies,
Of law, of loyalties
In which we live our days;
Inescapably part
Of our existence here
Where all who live must live
In this duality,
Worshipping Eros, yes,
The supple-waisted one
Quickener, giver of life,
But complicit also with
The hooded Thanatos
The lord of wilfulness
And the pit of Nothingness;
Who, however much they deplore,
In well-used cliché and phrase,
The abominable, strange
Accusative visitation,
Which our old city suffers,
And speak of a different, other

World which would find new ways
To rid itself of the beast,
Hidden away in its maze;
Know that we all exist
In symbiosis with
The dark thing in its lair,
Which belongs here, as do we,
As native as ourselves,
Breathing the summer air.

WHY?

Why does my heart not beat as theirs?
Asked the little boy as he stood on the stairs.

Why can I not rejoice in it all?
When I hear the laughter and pause in the hall?

Why did I not have equivalent fun?
On his way home asked the lonely one.

Why did I not enjoy their game?
Is it something in me that is always to blame?

Why can I never be really there,
Uncaringly as the others are?

Why am I always apart and thinking?
Why is it my heart is so often sinking?

I laugh and cheer as the others do.
I am one of the gang now, just like you;

I sing the songs in such unison
You would never think I was quite alone;

But I'm not really one of them anywhere:
In the dance, in the sports, in the fun of the fair,

Not one of them even beneath the moon
In the summer night when the roses bloom.

O let me be one of them somehow soon.

BOYS PLAYING FOOTBALL

Three little boys are playing with a football
Outside my window.
Scarcely more than toddlers,
They are dreaming perhaps
Of playing for Manchester United,
Or just allaying the deep interior boredom
Of dullard children.
They have now been joined
By what seems to be a fond parent.
Head as empty as the ball,
Like all inadequate personalities
He delights in being the instructor.
I hate the thud, thud against the wall,
The force, the scuffling, the cries,
The banality of the scene.
I reflect that the ball, a well-known brand,
Bought by the fond parent
Was probably made in Pakistan
By little boys their age,
Scarcely more than toddlers,
Bent over lasts for fourteen hours a day,
Stitching and stretching
With no time to play,
And none of this hateful, displaced energy,
Their fingers, the bones
In their backs and shoulders
Already deformed.
When the liberals find out,
Probably through a television programme,
There will be an outcry.
The well-known brand
Will be forced to apologise,
Say it didn't know,
Close down the factory.
The fond parents of the little workers,
Their grandparents, they themselves,
Their younger brothers and sisters,
Even their in-laws,
Will starve. The well-known brand
Will place contracts in another country,

Bangladesh or Cambodia,
And employ other little boys,
Scarcely more than toddlers,
But the liberals will not know that
They will be pleased
By their own outcry.
They will not care
That whole extended Pakistani families
Are now starving.
The fond parent,
Who is probably a liberal,
Will buy a new ball
And will be pleased
That it is not made in that Pakistani factory.
Complacent as ever,
He will smile on his own children.
It is the way of liberals.
It is the way of the world.

AND THAT DAY IN EL DIVINO SALVADOR

And that day in El Divino Salvador
Looking at the old woman
In front of the famous high altar.
I thought again how demiurgic we all were,
How excessively creative,
And how the philosophers who interpreted
Were nothing to us who created.
For this old woman kneeling there
In the echoing knave
Amid the splendour of the baroque
Had taken out of her shrivelled,
Apparently empty self
Such yearnings for Power,
For Mercy, for Justice,
For an amplitude
Able to give Peace and Rest,
Even to the poor,
Even to the mothers and wives of men
And to all other struggling old women,
That when she had rolled It all up into one ball
And pushed It through the altar rails
And up on to the high altar in front of her,
Into the embossed gold tabernacle,
It was so Great, so Sweet,
So unendingly Just and Merciful and Wise
That she was bowed down in adoration before It.
Such Gods were in old women and timid girls
And awkward boys making their first communion
That when they got angry they frightened
Even the strong men in the café.
Even the military governor
In his smart green uniform with red shoulder tabs,
Sitting over his thin-stemmed glass of pale Galliano
In the pale uncertain winter sunlight
On the terrace of the Mirador
While his bodyguard waited apart,
Sometimes behaved a little bit better
Because of his grandmother's god.
Or, perhaps, worse.

THE INCARNATION

God so loved humanity
He actually sent
His dear and only Son to share
Its state of banishment,

Sending Him out of heaven down
To this imperfect earth;
And that is why, this time of year,
We celebrate this Birth,

This wondrous, happy advent, that
His Son came down to save
Us, sinful and unworthy, give
Us hope beyond the grave;

Redeem us from the dire effects
Of our first parents' Fall,
Cleansing anew all sinful souls
Who happily hear His call.

We know God knew before He sent
His Son to us down here
What human life was really like,
The hunger, hurt and fear,

The calumny, betrayal, pain,
The agony and death,
The terrors that await all those
Who draw a mortal breath;

And so are struck with wonder that
His Son should come to share
So far, so far from heaven,
All that we have to bear.

And grateful too, of course, although
A thought may come to mind:
If He so loved the world He made
And our poor human kind,

Why did He have to send His Son
To go through all of this
When He could have just redeemed us with
A simple, Godlike kiss?

Or could if He so loved us, whether
We deserved or not,
Have saved us with a single, simple,
Loving Godly thought?

OUR PUP BUTLER

I praise our pup, Butler,
Because he thinks play is the proper occupation of all beings,
Because he is an optimist of pleasure, constantly eager and
    expecting frolic,
Because he has no fear of the future, trusting always to
    Provision,
Because he is quicker than Correction and makes it seem
    foolish,
Because he is always forgiving and bounds back with the
    same rapture,
Because he makes no excuses and suffers no remorse, but
    accepts the blame and is joyful again,
Because he speaks with his eyes, and has no need of words,
Because he smiles and laughs with his tail instead of baring
    his teeth in the deceitful human way.
Because he is loving by nature and has no need to hide
    contempt or hatred,
Because when he is tired he stretches out or curls up and does
    not sit complaining,
Because he provides cheerful companionship at very small
    cost in destruction,
Because his hair is a soft fur in token of his desire to be
    fondled and petted,
Because he has four white paws which are too big for his
    body,
Because he races with his feet well under him,
Because he cocks his head on one side when he is puzzled,
Because he accepts Existence without curiosity or question,
Because he is ignorant of Bush and Saddam Hussein and has
    no concept of Bush or Saddam Hussein,
Because he is oblivious of Countries or Continents, Universes
    or Galaxies, Gods or Devils, Heavens or Hells,
Because he is our pup, Butler.

GUARDIANS

In Richmond Park as darkness falls,
The herd lies down to rest,
The stags, as every night, apart
To north and south and west:

Males who in grave and adult pride
Will keep the herd from harm,
Raising their heavy antlered heads
At any slight alarm.

A notice on the roadside gate
Warns of a cull at dawn.
With rifles men will come to kill,
Workmanlike, doe and faun.

The stags will look on helplessly
For all their strength and pride.
While coolly and uncaringly
Their care is brushed aside.

WILLIAM CONOR'S "THE RIVETERS"

Cloth-capped and in the street clothes that had been
A Sunday best for bandstands in the park,
The ship's side sheer above them, new-milled steel.

That blessed moment which all art imposes.
Before the war, before the troubles, or
Before our ma died and we went to granny's.

A disappointment to the puzzled left,
The workers of the world once burdened with
Dreams born amid the bourgeois biedermeyer
Or in the schoolyard as the hot tears started.
But, since it's Belfast, staunch and true defenders
Of privilege, religion, freedom, laws.

Good draughtsmanship recalls us to the facts.
They are using a pneumatic riveter.
One cracks a joke, the youngest's not amused.
Apprentices are usually the butt.
Men riveting. Men punching in the hours.
Men paying for hire purchase with their time.
Men taking some pride in a skill they'd learned.
Not noble proletarians nor even prods,
Not working for the red dawn or the grey.
Not builders of the future, though the ship,
Titanic, towers above them, plates in place
For who knows what, torpedoes, icebergs or
Some profit to the owners, after which
The breakers would dismantle it again.
The plates go back into some mill and issue
As new Toyotas for their sons to buy.

He drew them walking home in '41
Or anyway away from work, perhaps
A cool, dark pub and ready for a pint.
A War Artist by then, he had to give it
A title that would justify the fee
Of fifty quid, so called it The Home Front.
And faith. The Home Front, it is always there.
Before and after war and revolution
Though king or country may not greatly care.

THE TROUBLE WITH ALPHO QUEALLY

The trouble with Alpho Queally
Was that he was never really,
Wholeheartedly, indubitably,
One hundred per cent, there.
Of course he occupied a space in air
Shaped to his body from feet to hair;
And though they might notice he seemed preoccupied
Partly because he so often sighed,
Others thought that he was really,
No doubt about it, there,
As everybody else seemed to be where
They were supposed at that moment to be,
Chatting about the weather, going tee-hee,
Ranting about politics with heat
Or discussing bunions and the state of their feet,

But this was not so. He was present physically
And sympathetically
On social occasions
And during most conversations
He was as anxious as a clucking hen
About the feelings of the others
He was apparently with,
Both concerned and curious
About the where and the when.
But even if he expressed himself with vigour
Or, as was often the case,
Something approaching rigour,
And also, sadly,
And, if you like, reprehensibly,
On more tender occasions,
Romantic assignations,
Even during what is called intimacy,
However badly
He wanted to be completely
As well as sweetly
With somebody else,
Whatever his urgencies
And protestations,
He was oddly not there

He was otherwhere.
Where was he then?
Was he absent in mind?
Thinking great thoughts?
Day-dreaming, wool-gathering,
Imagining some place
Where he would rather be instead?
Say, snug at home in his own bed,
For example, or on the wind-blown top
Of Bray Head?
No, that is not it.
He was not absent in mind,
Not socially blind.
He was acutely conscious of the tableau
Or the little group by the window
Of which he seemed to be a part,
Indeed at the heart.
Or even of the role
He was playing in somebody else's evening,
Somebody of whom he was truly fond,
And with whom he wished to establish a bond.

It was rather that Alpho Queally
Was like those people you read of
In accounts of after-death experience.
Like them he was really
Floating apart,
Looking down from outside,
From a corner of the ceiling
Or from the top of the wardrobe
– Of course with a lot of feeling
About himself and others,
Not by any means indifference –
At where he seemed to be
But wasn't because he was floating
Anxiously free.

That is what he was like.
A man who has had a long series
Of after-death experiences
Rather than a life.

ART

Art is where I
Need not be I,
They, they,
Nor even you be you,

And art is where
That sky above
Need not be grey
But milky summer blue.

Where art is
There the artist may
Decide just what to do,
Just what should be
And what we see
And whether you come too.

And yet, where art is, neither is
It all just like child's play,
For wishes are
Not horses here
To carry griefs away,
Restore you to
The happy fold
Or change a rainy day.
You cannot use the story told
To have things your own way.

Art's glory is, in part, its truth,
If not to that or this,
To skies, to presences, to life
In all its heady mix.
We change things for a better view
Of their reality.
Conjunctions, absences, the lot,
Art alters so that we can see
Another strange veracity,
What could be and what not.

And art is strict
Will not be tricked

Into a summer's day.
Though grey and blue
Can interchange
And likewise blue and grey,
It isn't like a day-dream and
A simple wish won't do,
The facts, if grey
Concerning you
Cannot be wished away.
Children know well that day-dream is
A world away from art,
That when the real world intrudes
The dream-world falls apart.

So art will not permit that we
When tired of life's complexity
Should wish things otherway,
Retreat into the never was
Of lovely summer's day,
Where art is, world is,
Whether grey
Or even endless blue
Is for that work the aspect that
The artist free to choose and change
May choose again to view.

And where it is
Is not because
A more amenable they
A beggar upon horseback or
A sky no longer grey
Are more attractive things to think
Or make than what have you,
An absence at the heart of things
A sky no longer blue.

MEDITATION ON A CLARE CLIFF-TOP

A fine day after storm in County Clare.
The waves are snatching at King George's Head.
The short grass of the cliff fields being cropped
By bullocks with a placid eye, I walk
On dizzying heights above the thunderous caves;
Can look down on the gulls in spume-shot air,
America beneath me too, beyond
The curve of ocean covering the earth
And held like me by gravity. I lean,
Light blue opacity above, dark blue below,
My raincoat tented wide against the wind,
A balancer elate upon a height.

And soon the Atlantic sunset from the cliff.
I'm not one for description, but the rich
Red path to the horizon, the huge disk
Sinking it seems beyond an edge, the clouds
Flaring to crimson up above while dark
Waits to enshroud and curtain the whole show,
It makes me against reason feel a part
Of something of some huge significance,
Profound and fraught with meaning and for me.
Of course it's ludicrous it should induce
This feeling in me. Me, black dot on cliff,
The word is pantheist. The example Wordsworth.

Before he died astronomers had counted
Fifty thousand other suns out there.
Bessel discovered, using parallax,
That one, called Cygni, was some sixty million
Miles above his laurel-wreathed head.
He didn't let it phase him. Suns he said,
Using the plural, speaking as we know of
A presence that disturbed him with the joy
Of elevated thoughts, a sense sublime
Of something far more deeply interfused
That dwelt within the light of setting suns
And the round ocean and the living air.
And in, of course he said, the mind of man.

They've raised the ante since. It's not just suns
But galaxies, I think ten million million
Not to mind other bangs and universes
And universes too on top of that.
And since there are countless other solar systems
They tell us that there must be other planets
All with their sudden afterglows like this
– So beautiful that when you turn and look
It's like a gulp of wind to catch the breath.
And, they insist, there must be chaps like me
To walk on cliff-tops, even County Clares,
– Or if not chaps like me then legless beings
Far cleverer than us and on their way.

I somehow doubt it. Deep within the bone
I disbelieve that there is anywhere
Like this Clare cliff-top with its close-cropped grass,
Or any wind like this Atlantic wind
Or any beings like us, so blown about
With beauty, terror, mystery and wonder.
And if they haven't this, what do they have
That can transcend their doubtless mortal lot
And give them something they can call a soul
And make them interesting to you and me?

When I began to read first there was talk
Of life on other planets. Venus, Mars,
And even the poor old moon were said to have
Inhabitants who might one day arrive
In strange machines to trouble Wimbledon
And Surrey and such legendary places.
But now we know that we are quite alone
Within the solar rays. Jules Verne was wrong
And both the Well(e)s's, Orson and H. G.,
The men from Mars not there and no green men,
Venusians to give the Christians pause
With a strange message of another love,
Or Fabians cheer with factory laws undreamt.

We have zoomed through zeniths heretofore unknown
But now within our daring human fling,
Sending our best, the camera, the mike,

The bodiless, scooping, metal hands aloft,
Only to find there's no-one there at all.
Within the rays of our sun anyway
There's nothing "highly organised" but here,
Not even frog-spawn, lovely scum of life.
It's down now to bacteria lapping dust,
Dry work at best, mere anaerobes agasp,
And even these improbable, no
Sentience within the realms of ice
And in the gas clouds no great gas at all.

It may be even that we're quite alone
In this vast whistling gallery, a folly
On which we'll bounce our radio waves in vain
And vainly bounce our speculations too.
The odds against life anywhere are long:
A shimmering atmosphere like ours, a balance
Of breathable heat and cold, of wet and dry,
A sun a certain distance, neither more
Nor less, to fructify, not burn all life away,
Or fail to melt the envelope of ice.

I pick my steps going homeward in the dark
And keep as far as possible inland
In spite of restless bullocks on my flank.
Some of these fissures run in quite a way
And if you don't take care – say, thinking of
The mundane matters that afflict us all,
Or gazing at the star-pierced deep of sky
And musing on the planet Jupiter,
Whose air is pungent, poisonous ammonia,
Or Saturn, shrouded in storms of splintered ice,
You could easily wind up spiked on pointed rock
Or swept by swirling waves into a cave.

If we're alone, what then? Does that not make
This little earth of ours more precious still?
Our troubled human kind, inventive, lithe,
Ingenious, deceitful, precious also?
If there is no one else out there to talk to,
Argue with, fight and look to but ourselves.
We've company enough in all the beings

So various, so beautiful, so strange,
Who've been our victims and our friends so far.

Earth, water, fire and air Greek sages said.
It still seems that's the formula, a fine
Day your honour and the wave-torn cliffs of Clare,
Earth and its oceans home to myriads,
Whales, damselflies, jerboas, jumping mice,
Humped bison, hedgehogs, horses, yes, and bullocks,
Soft velvet clouds of migrant butterflies,
Grey polyps floating over churning sand,
And on the high brown veldt of Africa
The protozoa called Trypanosoma,
Which causes sleeping sickness, milling in
Together, where man toils, accommodates –
Man, gardener, builder, hunter, worshipper
Of buffalo and snake and kangaroo,
Who saw the stars, beneficent and pale,
As I see Venus now above the waves,
Low in the west, bright star of evening love.